RIZZO

ALSO BY FRED HAMILTON

Confessions of a Dirty Ballplayer

So Long, Joey

RIZZO

FRED HAMILTON

THE VIKING PRESS ‖ NEW YORK

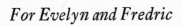

For Evelyn and Fredric

ACKNOWLEDGMENTS

A note of thanks to: Rolfe Neill, my boss, for permitting me to use material I had gathered on his time and not charging me a dime for doing it; Jon Katz, the best Rizzo-watcher in town; Charlie Montgomery, Frank Dougherty, and Joe O'Dowd, who collectively followed Car One for more than a decade; the patient folks in the library of Philadelphia Newspapers Inc.; Rich Aregood, a very wise man; Elwood P. Smith, a fine news photographer; Rita Oliva, who somehow managed to decipher my code and type the manuscript; the many people who gave of their knowledge about the subject, including Spencer Coxe, Jack Levine, James Tate, Thacher Longstreth, Richardson Dilworth, and others too numerous to mention, and several guys who wisely prefer to remain anonymous. They know who they are.

Contents

(*Illustrations follow page* 84)

RIZZO

I

Who Is Frank Rizzo and Why Is He Running Philadelphia?

It was only 6:30 p.m. and the polls wouldn't close for another hour and a half. But at the Bellevue-Stratford Hotel, Frank Rizzo's election headquarters, everything was just about ready.

Nearly one-fourth of the large, stately Red Room on the second floor had been roped off as a press area, where dozens of television lights mercilessly beat down on a small podium from which the candidate would accept his election as the Mayor of Philadelphia.

Out on Broad Street, across from the main entranceway of the hotel, there was a red police communication van. Dozens of cops in yellow raincoats milled about on the sidewalk and guarded the doors on Broad Street and around the corner on Walnut. At other various strategic locations nearby, police sat in unmarked vehicles smoking cigarettes and monitoring their radios.

In the hallways and corridors of the hotel plainclothesmen, detectives, and uniformed officers outnumbered the media representatives and the first contingent of well-wishers. They eyed anyone who looked suspicious and kept peering about for any packages that might contain a bomb.

John Lawrence, a tall, blond public relations man for the Democratic City Committee, was nervous. He was trying to help the newsmen set up and he was also busy checking credentials, seeing that each person wore a little white donkey on his lapel. Finally, bowing to the heat of the damnable lights, he moved toward an open window, pushed aside the heavy red drapery, and thrust his face into the cold damp air. Three breaths later he was interrupted.

"Why all the cops?" a reporter from New York asked him.

Lawrence, seemingly startled by the question, stared at his inquisitor and said condescendingly: "Now why the hell do you think? We don't want another Bobby Kennedy here."

The reporter shrugged and walked away. Lawrence looked perturbed.

"Can you believe a guy would ask a goddamn fool question like that?" he asked. He then turned and headed toward his office on Walnut Street. There were more credentials to be checked, more white donkeys to be handed out.

"Jesus," he could be heard muttering as he passed through the doors shaking his head. "Unbelievable."

A M Y K E L L E Y W O U L D make or break this night. The attractive middle-aged woman with neatly coiffured blond hair would be the first person in the private suite to know how well, or how poorly, Frank Lazzaro Rizzo was running.

She sat at a small desk, ear glued to the telephone. At the other end of the line, in the computer center at the Municipal Services Building some four blocks away, was Albert V. Gaudiosi, the man who for ten long months as manager of the very low-key campaign had muted the most forceful voice in Philadelphia.

Amy held a rigid secretarial pose, scratching figures on a

yellow legal pad. Division by division, ward by ward, she wrote down the numbers. Periodically, she would give a running total. Each time she did, Rizzo would smile.

"Look at South Philadelphia," he shouted above the cocktail chatter. Amy had just penned the results of Ward 1, Division 1, which gave Rizzo, 439; Thacher Longstreth, 98.

"It's all over; I'll have another drink now," Rizzo said, and he was handed a gin and tonic before the slice of lime could hit the bottom of the glass.

The figures being compiled came as no surprise to anyone in the suite that cold, rainy night of November 2, 1971. It was just about what they had expected, what they had been confident of throughout the long, dreary campaign. Indeed, if an emotional element was missing it was that transmittable feeling of apprehension that can lay siege to people whose lives depend upon an event over which they no longer have influence or control.

In this suite on the third floor of the stately Bellevue-Stratford, one could sense an attitude of smugness that bordered on the blasé. It was personified in the central figure at this gathering, the man whose amazing career would be catapulted to new heights or abruptly brought to an embarrassing end by the neatly written numbers on Amy Kelley's legal pad. Rizzo was unusually quiet, but not nervous. The room was warm, but he looked cool. His hair, shiny black and parted high on the right side, was slick as a wet seal's, with every strand in place. Poised, even dignified, he greeted new arrivals with a warm, strong handshake, occasionally interrupting his easy conversation to peer over the secretary's shoulder and check the returns. Each time he did, he would smile and draw heavily from his filter-tipped cigarette.

"I'm leading by twenty-five thousand," he said at one point to Leonard Tose, the owner of the Philadelphia Eagles, who, almost giddy and clearly out of place, responded frankly, "Is that good? I'm not a politician, you know."

In an adjoining room of the suite, some twenty of Rizzo's faithful casually sipped drinks. There was a steady din of chatter, but no cheering or shouting. Hands were shaken, introductions were made, and there was some winking and nodding and subtle talk of the future—vague hints of spoils to be distributed.

At 9 p.m., the returns showed Rizzo with a slowly building lead of about 40,000. Peter J. Camiel, the heavy-set, moon-faced chairman of the Democratic Party City Committee was beaming. His men in the wards had performed well. Although Rizzo's lead would never hit the 90,000 margin he had predicted and hoped for, he would still win it and Democrats were being swept into the all-important City Council seats.

Rizzo put down his glass, adjusted his coat, and turned to a small group that included his son, Francis, Tose, and several reporters.

"About time to go down, right?"

The crowd quickly backed up, opening a path to the door, which was guarded by a uniformed policeman. It was opened, and the party quickly moved down the hallway to the staircase at the bottom of which was assembled a tightly compressed mob of perspiring, wildly enthusiastic supporters. As Rizzo's shiny black shoes became visible from the bottom of the stairs, a middle-aged woman fairly dripping with make-up surged forward, her great breasts nearly exploding from the low-cut evening dress.

"Here he comes, here he comes," she shrieked and pandemonium broke loose.

Two doors down the street at the old Keystone Building, things were considerably more subdued. W. Thacher Longstreth, the tall, lanky Republican, was ensconced in a room on the fifth floor, from which all but his family and closest associates had been barred. Three floors below, a pall was beginning to settle over the crowd that only two hours before had been excitedly optimistic.

As the first returns showed Rizzo leading, a local radio station predicted his election. A television program was interrupted to announce that the Associated Press was calling it a Rizzo victory.

"No, I can't believe that," a girl said. "It's too early."

But this faint optimism soon gave way to reality, and a feeling of emptiness began to settle in. Months of work, hundreds of thousands of dollars were slowly being decimated. Rizzo's political juggernaut rolled on, and as it passed, it left them almost lifeless. They stood quietly, expressionless. Longstreth's supporters waited for their candidate to come forth and say it wasn't true. But it was very true and the sounds drifting in from the street below told them so.

The cops at the Bellevue-Stratford had all but given up. The crowd had swelled beyond all expectations. It filled the Red Room, spilled over into the hallway, down the steps into the lobby, and finally out onto the sidewalks and streets. Even the Poor Richard Room, a small anteroom adjoining the main banquet hall that had been set aside for members of the Rizzo party, was wall-to-wall pushing, shoving bodies.

It took Rizzo twenty minutes to walk the fifty feet from the staircase, through the Poor Richard Room, and to the podium in the press area of the Red Room. Hands reached out from all directions to touch him. Women tried to kiss him and the sweat began to roll down his cheeks and forehead, only to be whisked away by the incessant swipes of a white linen handkerchief.

At 9:20, with the roar of his admirers engulfing him, Rizzo climbed triumphantly up the steps of the podium, followed by his brother Joseph, Camiel, and several reporters and aides.

Rizzo called out to Philadelphia reporters by name, and

they acknowledged him with a sheepish grin as their colleagues from other cities observed in bewilderment the lack
of formality. After several minutes of handshaking, the noise
died down somewhat in the expectation that he would make
a victory statement. But it was not forthcoming.

Rizzo wanted first to hear that Longstreth had conceded.
He wanted his opponent to admit defeat before he gloated
over his own victory. He discussed this briefly with Camiel,
who turned to Gaudiosi and instructed him to call Longstreth headquarters and kindly inquire if the Republican was
going to throw in the towel, the outcome now clear and it
being so damned hot.

Gaudiosi forced his way through the mob. He returned
several minutes later. The three men then huddled on the
podium.

"He's going to make a concession speech in about seven
minutes," Gaudiosi whispered. "And he wants to come over
here afterward and make a speech for unity."

Rizzo stared down at his faithful campaign manager, then
looked at Camiel, and finally replied in a low, deep-rolling
voice: "Fuck him."

So the wait continued, until shortly before 10 p.m., when
the incumbent mayor, James Hugh Joseph Tate, a sixty-one-
year-old silver-haired Irishman who had run the city for ten
years, came pushing through the Bellevue-Stratford crowd,
accompanied by his wife, Anne. Tate perhaps more than
Rizzo himself appreciated the magnitude of the moment.
There were those who said this old warrior was the embodiment of the "Peter Principle." There were those, including his underlings, who said he was a tyrant, a self-serving political boss who demanded homage. But whatever they
said, tonight he was vindicated. He had put his tired old
political machine into one last lap on the election track and
it had won going away.

And as Tate turned to the microphones to let these people

know it, someone monitoring one of the televisions in the room screamed out, "He's conceded, he's conceded."

The shouts of victory became near deafening.

Longstreth had every right to be bitter. Twice scorned by the voters and sapped of energy, he would have found few to blame him for lashing out one last time.

"But that's the way the ball bounces," he somberly told his followers. "There comes a time in every campaign when the winner wins, and the loser loses. I offer him my congratulations and I offer him my support. Mayor Rizzo needs the support of everyone and I hope to give it to him. We must give him our support. . . ."

"No way," they cried out. "No way."

It was time for tears but none were visible behind Longstreth's horn-rimmed glasses.

"I'm too big to cry," he said almost whimsically, "and it hurts too much to smile."

He left the Keystone Building like a gentleman. At the Bellevue-Stratford, it was something else. The Rizzo people there hauled out a mock casket and carried it into the street. The manikin feet protruding from the end of the casket were encased in argyle socks, Longstreth's trademark. And they howled and cheered and heckled his supporters, many of whom answered in kind. There would be no physical clash, however; 150 cops would see to that. Nor would there be trouble out in the neighborhoods. Eleven buses carrying 500 policemen would make sure of it.

And certainly no disparaging word could be heard in the Bellevue-Stratford. Mayor-Elect Frank Rizzo had kissed his wife and he had now moved up to the microphones, arms outstretched in a sign of victory.

"Only in America could a guy like Frank Rizzo be elected mayor," he said. "My first job is to bring this entire community back together again and make this a better city for all the people."

He had at least conceded that the city was divided along racial lines and perhaps this in itself was a first step toward turning things around. But election night was a time for celebration. The problems would be there tomorrow, and the next day, and probably for the next four years. No need to worry about them now.

Downtown, as they call South Philadelphia, had gone bananas. Not since the Phillies had won the pennant back in 1950 had Little Italy turned on to such a celebration. They poured into the streets by the thousands, dancing and cheering. Many took to their cars and went horn-honking up and down Broad Street. Still others, not wishing to fight the street crowds, waved red-green-and-white flags from the second-floor windows of their row houses.

And why not? Rizzo was one of them. He was a *paesano*, the first of his nationality to be elected Mayor of Philadelphia although 109 men had held the position before him. And Frank Rizzo was no wispy, aristocratic northerner. He was every inch a Calabrese, with a round nose, pudgy features, swarthy skin, pasta girth, and a fiery Latin temperament.

But more than that, he had been born and raised among them, the son of an immigrant up from poverty. He knew what it meant to live on the block, to suffer through the stagnant heat of summer in a "Father, Son, and Holy Ghost," row house—three rooms stacked upon one another with no cross ventilation. He knew how quickly the fan melted the cake of ice and how tough it was to get coal.

Frank Rizzo knew as well as any of them what it was to be called "guinea," "greaser," and "wop"; he had become as furious as they had, striking out with his fists and driving them home on the fury of past offenses against his heritage.

Rizzo had become their vicarious offering, the *machismo maximus*. So he lacked the polish of noble breeding; what could that get you? A limp wrist and a one-man show at a gallery? A shirt with your name on the label? Better *boccie* balls if it meant the big chair in the hall. The slogan "Kiss Me, I'm Italian" had taken on a whole new meaning in Philadelphia.

Of greater significance, however, was the fact that Frank Rizzo had emerged as the unchallenged leader of a new force in Philadelphia politics: a heretofore unlikely coalition of ethnic groups held together by the color of their skin—white—and a common emotion—fear.

That race was a key issue in the campaign is hardly disputable, although Rizzo himself never advocated racist or segregationist policies. Quite simply, Rizzo, by virtue of his image as a "supercop," had become anathema to most blacks. The voting patterns clearly established that; he carried only one of twenty-two predominantly black wards. Rizzo was elected mayor by an ethnic conglomerate of Italians in South Philadelphia, Irish and Poles in the white working- and middle-class neighborhoods, and the Jews of Oxford Circle and Overbrook. The blacks, the liberals, and the young—party registration not withstanding—came out against him.

It was the first time in memory that the city's black voters had turned their backs on the Democratic Party, which for so many years had taken them for granted and had given them so little. Thus a second major political force came into being in 1971—a large independent block of black voters who having ignored tradition would not be likely to fall in line again on the strength of empty promises and pint bottles of cheap wine.

Rizzo's call to law and order ("You get them to the electric chair, I'll throw the switch myself") played upon the very real fears shared alike by young and old, rich and poor. But it was particularly effective among the white working classes whose neighborhoods border on the black ghettos and who care little about the social conditions that give rise to crime or long-range economic and rehabilitative programs that might eradicate those conditions.

"Rizzo Right Now" and "Rizzo Means Business," two of his campaign slogans, plucked at the fibers of this fear. He wanted them to know that his solutions to the crime problem were not those of a glib-tongued liberal who was always talking about the rights of the accused. He offered pragmatic, even simplistic solutions: hire 2000 more cops (although the city was already $60 million in the red and he had promised no increase in taxes), get rid of the "lenient judges who turn wild animals loose on the streets," reactivate the mounted patrolmen in business districts, legalize all forms of gambling and make the winnings tax free, give stiffer penalties to all criminals, and one of his top priorities, clean out the death rows by switching on the juice to the electric chair.

To many of his followers, the issues of race and law and order were synonymous. Their attitudes could be summed up roughly as follows: keeping the colored in their place would take care of law and order; if they want to kill, rape, and rob one another, as the statistics showed they were doing, let them. But not in Kensington, or Fishtown, or Two Street. God forbid. Or Frank Rizzo forbid, and since the Good Lord seemed to have forsaken them, why not give Rizzo a shot at it?

On the face of it, Rizzo should not have won the election. Longstreth outspent him, outcampaigned him, and had a broader base of support. He also was more articulate, better versed in city government, and had compiled an impressive list of endorsements from the news media, civic leaders, and national and local politicians of both parties. Moreover, Rizzo's own party was hopelessly split between conservative and liberal elements, and he had been forced throughout the campaign to walk hand-in-hand with Jim Tate, a most unpopular lame duck.

In spite of it all, Longstreth lost by almost 50,000 votes. Had he won by the same margin, he could have claimed a mandate. But Rizzo could not; his constituency, however vociferous and loyal, was monolithic. Thus the city, as it had been throughout the years Rizzo ran the police department, remained sharply divided along racial and class lines.

The fact that he was elected mayor, however, did more than make him the political leader of Philadelphia; it placed him at the threshold of becoming a major force in the National Democratic Party.

Philadelphia gave John F. Kennedy, Lyndon B. Johnson, and Hubert H. Humphrey wide margins of victory—enough to win them the entire state, the nation's fourth largest in population and electoral votes.

Whether Rizzo could have transferred his own popularity to that of the Democratic candidate is a matter of conjecture since he had not welded together the kind of machine that can deliver a bloc of votes *à la* Richard J. Daley of Chicago.

But this question became academic in the spring of 1972 because Rizzo, as has come to be expected, did the unexpected. Several weeks before the Pennsylvania Democratic primary in May 1972, he publicly announced that Richard Nixon was "one of the greatest Presidents in the history of our country," and that he, Rizzo, was going to vote for him in November.

"I'm a Democrat and I'm not going to tell people to vote Republican," Rizzo said. "But I am telling them that I'm voting for the President."

Prior to this, Rizzo had been courted by Senator Hubert Humphrey, Senator George McGovern, and Senator Henry Jackson (the latter being the only Democratic candidate who came close to suiting Rizzo philosophically). Indeed, on the night he was elected, Rizzo received a congratulatory telephone call from Humphrey, and Senator Edmund S. Muskie sent along his best wishes the following day. But Rizzo had proved to be a fickle political mate by endorsing Nixon. By

Who Is Frank Rizzo? || 13

the time the primary was over, his chances of wielding political power in the national party, by his own design, were shot.

"I hope McGovern gets it on the first ballot," Rizzo laughingly said at least a dozen times. "It'll make it that much easier for the President to be elected."

All of which clearly illustrates Rizzo's fierce independence, his reluctance to be beholden to anyone. He felt quite comfortable supporting Nixon. The President's philosophy on any number of issues, including law and order, welfare, busing, and racial matters closely paralleled his own. And he felt confident that Nixon would be re-elected in November, thus enhancing his prospects of getting more federal money into Philadelphia.

Beyond these matters, however, lies the intriguing fact that Rizzo's election in 1971 was among the first evidences of the rise of neopopulism in the United States.

Rizzo projected himself as a common man of simple words. He played upon the fears and frustrations of the increasingly silent majority by hammering away at the issues of crime, inflation, the erosion of traditional values and social mores, the ineptitude and wastefulness of bureaucracy, the decline of red-blooded patriotism, welfare fraud, and "give-away" programs. He was against busing to achieve racial desegregation and said that government-subsidized housing was a failure. He promised to help the low- and middle-income citizens by giving them better services and not raising their taxes, and he pledged to bring more businesses into the city to stimulate the economy.

In fact, Rizzo's campaign style and rhetoric bore a striking similarity to that of Governor George C. Wallace of Alabama, a man he personally disliked and the man who, along with McGovern, brought neopopulism into full bloom during the 1972 Presidential campaign.

Rizzo blanches at the thought of being compared to Wallace; the latter, he feels, has gone beyond the pale of ethical and moral legitimacy. He will remind those who make such comparisons that it was he, Frank Rizzo, who called the Alabama State House in 1968 in an attempt to persuade Wallace from coming to Philadelphia because racial tensions were running high.

Yet the similarity definitely is there, although it must be said that the two men are far apart on the issue of race. Rizzo is not a segregationist. While he frequently was charged with heightening racial tensions, there were many instances in which he actually cooled them.

Rizzo's election showed that he was, as he has so often been, a man for the times. A war-weary citizenry, feeling the pinch of inflation, and that even the sanctuary of their social institutions was being challenged, had found in Rizzo the embodiment of their own feelings and ideas. He wanted to "get things back to the middle," where he and his followers felt safe and secure, where the values and ideals to which they tenaciously were clinging would be preserved. He was aware of the anxieties and he exploited them by pushing Philadelphians to the brink of frustration and then snatching them away just in the nick of time. Not through firebrand rhetoric did he arouse them (he had forsaken that when he stepped down as police commissioner); his manner was more in the form of street vernacular, talking to his followers in an easy, often humorous way. Rizzo allied their common fears and gave credence to their own misgivings about the world, the nation, and their city. He reinforced the idea that their simplistic solutions to complex problems were the right solutions because, after all, they were his, too.

"I don't know what the answer to the education problem is," he would say quite seriously. Then, smiling, he would quickly add, "But the ones they're using now aren't working.

Maybe we ought to go back to the old days, you know, you write all As one day, all Bs the next . . . at least you learned the ABCs."

And they would laugh and applaud; somewhere deep inside they felt he was probably right.

The popularity of Wallace and McGovern in 1972 was ample evidence that the attitudes of Philadelphia voters were not unlike those of voters throughout the country. There is not one or even several local issues upon which Rizzo's victory could be hinged, not even his pledge to hold the line on taxes. That promise had been made by Mayor Tate, and it had been broken. Rather, Rizzo was the whole, a much greater whole than the sum of his parts. His popularity, therefore, extended far beyond the city limits.

During the campaign, Rizzo had contracted Oliver Quayle to poll his popularity in New Jersey and Pennsylvania. He never made public the results of those polls, nor did he even let it be known that he had had them taken. After six months in office he said in an interview:

"I ran better there [both states] than I did in Philadelphia. They talk about power. My power's not with the politicians. It comes from the people."

Thus the question often heard is what will Rizzo do in 1976, or, if he seeks and wins a second term, in 1980? It is necessary to look beyond the man to find the answer because the elements of ambition and ego—and in his own mind, at least, the call to destiny—are clearly present. He has already hinted several times that he might run for governor, but that would depend on whether District Attorney Arlen Specter seeks the Republican nomination, which appears likely. (Rizzo has said many times he would not run against the DA.) Beyond that, only Rizzo himself may know, and it is safe to say that even he is not quite sure.

In any event, Rizzo's political future depends as much upon the mood of the voters as upon his success or failure as mayor. If law and order, inflation, a general disenchantment with the political leadership, and the upheaval of the social structure are as prevalent then as they are now, he conceivably could become a national political power. If not, his future could be in doubt. But this is far from the last word.

As his opponents have discovered, it is easy to underestimate Frank L. Rizzo. Those who have done so have come up woefully short. This high-school dropout is a man of enormous energy and resourcefulness—clever, in some instances, to the point of brilliance; cunning to the point of danger. He is neither to be dismissed as a happenstance of time and event, nor to be analyzed to predictability.

For these reasons, Rizzo remains something of a mystery even to those who know him well. Each time one peers beneath the surface of this formidable man, a new facet seems to appear, a light-giving surface that, depending on one's point of view, radiates fear or admiration, alarm or comfort.

II

Up from Little Italy

The three old Italian men stood on the corner of 15th and
Wolf Streets talking with their hands while the temperature
that January day in 1971 pushed toward forty degrees. Two
of the men were considerably larger than the third, their
swollen stomachs thrusting through their heavy, wool over-
coats. The third man was short and thin, almost tiny. His
deep-set eyes were surrounded by webs of wrinkles and his
battered fedora was pushed back on his head. He reached
into his pocket, withdrew a small pocketknife and, as he
began cleaning his fingernails, told about the time forty
years ago when a black man had attempted to hold up his
South Philadelphia butcher shop.

The robber had walked up to the counter and demanded
that a butcher open the cash drawer, put the money in a
bag, and hand it over. The butcher, seeing the man's drawn
pistol, promptly obeyed. When the black man turned to
leave, the owner, who had been listening from the back
room, angrily emerged with a meat cleaver.

"Dat-a no good son-of-a-beetch," the little man said, making a sweeping vertical motion with the pocketknife. "I hit-a

him between the shoulders and he split open like a water-melon, top-a to bottom."

The little man and the butcher threw the black man's body on a scrap-meat truck. Police found it the next day, and the case, following a cursory investigation that produced no arrests, was closed.

"We take-a no shit in them days," the little man added as his two friends wiped the tears of laughter from their eyes.

PHILADELPHIA is a sprawling metropolis in southeastern Pennsylvania situated on the west bank of the Delaware River. New Jersey is on the opposite shore. Almanacs describe it as the "City of Brotherly Love," the "Birthplace of the Nation," and William Penn's "town." According to the 1970 census, 1,950,098 residents live within its 129 square miles. Geography books list it as the nation's fourth largest city, a center for industry, shipping, finance, scholarship, and medicine.

Although technically correct, these statistics are somewhat misleading. They imply that the city is an entity, a single municipality. Legally, it is, but for all practical purposes, it is necessary to consider Philadelphia as a loose confederation of separatist neighborhoods, each with a distinct life-style reflecting ethnic, race, and income levels—each commanding loyalties superior to those accorded the city proper. Where they are not legally bound, the neighborhoods have little in common.

There is Schuylkill, for example, an Irish neighborhood known originally as Out Schuylkill and named for the river that flows by its western boundary. Schuylkill is a quaint, blue-collar district at the western extremity of the center-city business district. Originally settled by Irish laborers in the early nineteenth century, it remains Irish today, with third and fourth generations of the same families living in houses built by their forefathers more than a century ago.

North of center city, along the banks of the Delaware, is Kensington, a mill-town neighborhood inhabited by white lower-income and lower-middle-income families who work in neighborhood factories, mills, and warehouses. Residents of Kensington are predominantly Polish, German, English, and Irish, and the neighborhood is a city in itself. Most Kensingtonians own their own homes, shop local stores, belong to neighborhood fraternal organizations and civic groups, and socialize among themselves in neighborhood restaurants and taprooms. Kensington's primary concern at this point in its long history is the threat of a black migration from the neighboring North Philadelphia ghetto. Running a close second is law and order, which explains why Frank Rizzo is a folk hero in Kensington.

There are seemingly countless other neighborhoods—Fishtown, Two Street, East Falls, Powelton Village, Chestnut Hill, Germantown, to name a few—each with a unique character, each generating intense loyalty from its residents. Asked where he's from, a Philadelphian usually will preface the name of his city with that of his neighborhood, unless he lives in South Philadelphia. In that case he has said enough, because the odds are good that he will either be an Italian from Little Italy or a Negro from the northern ghetto section of South Philadelphia.

Like much of the city, South Philadelphia's narrow streets are lined with adjoining two- and three-story brick row houses that run the length of an entire block. Houses on each block and sometimes in whole neighborhoods are of the same design, forming a monotonous architecture that is interrupted only occasionally by a factory, school, church, or vacant lot. By standing on the roof of almost any one of these row houses it is possible to see the rest of South Philadelphia sweep out to the horizon almost like the corn fields of Kansas and Iowa.

There's little that distinguishes the homes of Little Italy from houses in, say, North Philadelphia, except that their exteriors are well maintained and the streets, sidewalks, steps, and landings are cleaned daily. The women of Little Italy seem never to tire of toiling over their parcel of concrete and asphalt with a scrubbing brush, broom, or hose.

The simple exteriors of these row houses frequently belie the lavish interiors, however. Great velvet-covered chairs and sofas adorn the pile-carpeted living rooms. Windows, hidden from the inside by lace curtains, are hooded on the outside by aluminum awnings. Sculptured lamps and imitation Ming vases adorn the coffee tables. And there's usually a Madonna, a picture or tapestry of John F. Kennedy, and a plastic-framed color print of Pope John XXIII.

Attempts at remodeling the bland exteriors of the row houses have been unsuccessful for the most part. Artificial stone, usually of a brackish gray color, has been attached to the bricks of some of the houses. While such renovation speaks of new prosperity, a house that has it stands out like acne. Some residents have applied white paint to the mortar between the bricks. Others have painted the entire fronts of the houses. But the vast majority of the row houses in South Philadelphia look much the same today as they did fifty years ago, when many of them were built.

The charm and character of Little Italy, however, are found in things far less tangible than the design and décor of the homes and the Italian propensity for cleanliness. They are evident in the Italo-American life-style of which South Philadelphia is the very essence—the industriousness, gusto, and mannerisms of the people; their lustiness, bravado, family loyalty, and ethnic pride. It is reflected in the history of this colorful neighborhood, the struggle of its people to raise themselves from the poverty and misery they found upon immigrating to this country. And it is epitomized by its native sons who found success, men like Mario Lanza, Al

Martino, Bobby Rydell, Buddy Greco, Frankie Avalon, a flash-in-the-pan singer named Fabian, and, of course, Francis Lazzaro Rizzo.

Philadelphia's Italian ghetto once took in almost all of South Philadelphia. It spread from South Street, the southern boundary of center city, down to the Navy Yard, and it took in most of the area between the Delaware and Schuylkill Rivers. Scattered throughout this large area were pocket settlements of Jews, Irish, and Lebanese, and there was a black community around South Street. In a narrow corridor along the Delaware River, a neighborhood known as Two Street still thrives. It is a mixed bag of nationalities, traditionally the home of the sailors and longshoremen who work on the docks of the sprawling port. At the turn of the century, however, South Philadelphia was one of the largest Italian settlements in the country.

In *The Private City: Philadelphia in Three Periods of Its Growth** Sam Bass Warner, Jr., described South Philadelphia's social role in the metropolis as: "a port of entry for poor immigrants and Negroes, and as a refuge for the poor of the city in general."

> Although large numbers of South Philadelphia's immigrants and poor worked in the service trades and loft manufacturing establishments on the edge of the downtown, the district was screened off from the downtown by its northern margin of sin and slums. The cramped streets and alley housing of the blocks between the Spruce and South Streets had served as the Negro ghetto and a white slum for a century (by 1930). Here, and on adjacent downtown streets, the police concentrated the gambling, prostitution and speakeasies of the city. Moreover, because South Philadelphia was a peninsula, no middle-class commuters passed through the district on their way to outer suburbs.
>
> Isolation from the main flow of Philadelphia life, however,

* Philadelphia: University of Pennsylvania Press, 1968.

helped the neighborhoods of South Philadelphia maintain a separate identity. Isolation bred parochialism and the shelter of insulated ghettos within which, at least when he returned home at night, the newcomer could learn American urban culture while living among his fellow beginners with whom he shared a common experience, language, and church.

South Philadelphia prior to the Civil War had been little more than a sparsely settled suburb. Seventy-five years later, it had an Italian population of 175,000. By almost any standard the growth rate was phenomenal, and Lorenzo Nardi, the man who started it, could be considered something of a second Columbus. Nardi came to Philadelphia from Italy in 1852 and searched for a week before he found a fellow countryman. Thirty years later, he had succeeded in luring some twenty Italian families to South Philadelphia where they settled in cramped quarters along Montrose Street between 6th and 10th Streets. Nardi also formed the Unione Fratellanze, the first of dozens of fraternal and political organizations that would spring up through the years.

At the turn of the century, the Italian population of South Philadelphia had exploded to 100,000, and more were streaming in daily. The social clubs and fraternities numbered almost 100, and Nardi's Unione Fratellanze had 1200 members. Twenty years later, when the great migration from Italy had tapered off, South Philadelphia's Little Italy was home for 150,000, and its citizens had staked out a permanent claim in the city's government, professional, and business circles.*

The growth of the district had followed two general patterns. Immigrants from Italy usually tried to move near their relatives or friends. Failing that, they took up residence in areas that were inhabited by Italians from their same town or region. So there would be entire streets comprised of one family, its relatives and friends, and whole neighborhoods

* Public Ledger, May 15, 1927.

of Calabrese, Genovese, Albanese, Napolitanos, and Sicilianos.

The open-air market on 9th Street between Passyunk Avenue and Christian Street is probably the last vestige of the Victorian era Little Italy. It was here that it all began (Montrose Street runs smack through it), and it is here that the old-timers and those who have since moved away come back to find their memories among the vegetable stands, kegs of olive oil, tattered awnings, and cobblestone streets.

Fifty years ago, 9th Street was Philadephia's Les Halles. It was the focal point of the Italian community, its shopping district, and its social center—a cacophony of sounds. The squealing of goats, sheep, and pigs being slaughtered fused with the shouts of husky women driving a bargain. On the street were the hawkers, the pushcart vendors, and the mobs of people; women carrying baskets on their heads, men holding their tools and lunch pails in their hands. Children ran through the streets playing "dead box" and stickball, and everywhere was the aroma arising from huge wheels of provolone and romano or the cooking of garlic-laced tomato sauce.

Trolleys and horse-drawn wagons crawled through the street while men around the taprooms fought political battles and played "more," or "fingers."

There was little in the way of necessities that couldn't be purchased on 9th Street. Furniture, clothing, food, and wine —it was all there for the bargaining and the buying. It was, as it is now, a bit of the old world in the new one, only then it was more vibrant, more typical of the neighborhood lifestyle. And it was during this period, when Little Italy was in its heyday, 1908, that a fifteen-year-old boy named Rafael Rizzo first set foot in Philadelphia. He had come alone to this country from Chiaravalle Centrale, Catanzaro, in Calabria, where his father had been a Garibaldi freedom fighter. Like most immigrants, he carried visions of a better life in America. Also, like most immigrants, he was practically penniless. Rafael carried what he owned in his bags and what little money he had in his pocket.

Rafael's only connection in this country was with a family living in South Philadelphia, old friends of his family in Calabria. They met the boy when he arrived in Philadelphia and offered him a place to stay, but he chose to live alone in an apartment at 8th and Kater Streets, just below South Street, where the area was still predominantly Italian.

Rafael was a tailor. He looked for work at several factories and clothiers', finally landing a job at Jacob Reed's Sons men's store on Chestnut Street, within walking distance of his house. He worked under a score of journeymen tailors; the salary was small and he came to realize that his future there was limited. A short time later, he opened his own tailoring shop at 5th and South Streets, where he fared slightly better. Rafael Rizzo was not an exceptionally ambitious young man. He did not dream of acquiring wealth or position. He wanted a job that paid a living wage and one that would permit him to save toward retirement. In short, he wanted security, an elusive commodity for men who had fled the poverty and instability of their mother countries.

Beyond that was the matter of finding a wife who would bear him children. Italians in those days were strong believers in the family as an economic and social unit, the larger and more close-knit the family, the better. Rafael, alone in America and separated from his family by an ocean, longed for a wife and children of his own. But he felt he must first be able to support a family, and it was obvious to him that tailoring was not the kind of work that would do it. In these pre–World War I days, the most secure and dependable employment was being offered by the government. Trolley drivers, mailmen, firemen, and policemen all seemed to be working steadily without fear of losing their jobs. They were uniformed and secure, earning living wages, and the requirements for these jobs were minimal.

So in 1914, at the age of twenty-one, Rafael Rizzo put away his needle and thread and became the first Italian to be sworn into the Philadelphia Police Department, the nation's oldest. The Irish, who years before had sought the same kind of security behind the badge that Rizzo hoped he would find, were in control of the department. They called Rafael "Ralph."

Ralph was assigned to the South Philadelphia neighborhood around 8th and Fitzwater Streets. Because he was Italian, he made friends quickly, and was consulted as a lawyer, doctor, and marriage counselor. It was on Fitzwater Street that he met Teresa Erminio, a kind and gentle girl who had been born of immigrant parents in Philadelphia. They dated a short while and then married, moving to Rizzo's house on 8th and Kater Streets. The neighborhood then was beginning to undergo the social and economic changes that have been pushing back the boundaries of Little Italy ever since.

As Negro families began settling in the predominantly Italian areas south of South Street, the Italians began moving away. Some fled to other areas of the city; some crossed the Delaware and settled in New Jersey. Those who stayed retreated south into the entrenched Italian areas. The result was that Little Italy diminished in size, but remained an all-white, almost all-Italian enclave and was able to preserve its ethnic life-style. Meanwhile, the South Street district became the gathering place for hoodlums, gamblers, and bootleggers —the street men and lieutenants of the city's first organized crime leaders, James "Big Jim" Nazone, Anthony "Musky" Zanghi, and John "Big Nose" Avena.

The Rizzos, like hundreds of other Italian families, moved to the quieter residential districts of South Philadelphia. They made a down payment on a house at 2322 South Rosewood

Street, a narrow, alleylike street that runs parallel to and a block west of Broad Street, one of the city's main thoroughfares. On October 23, 1920, Teresa Rizzo gave birth to the first of four sons, Francis Lazzaro; soon to follow were Ralph, Jr., Joseph, and Anthony.

The street, or block, was a social institution when "Franny," as Francis's father called him, was growing up on South Rosewood Street. Not only were the individual families close-knit, but groups of families on the same street maintained close relationships. When the men went to work in the morning at the factories, mills, construction jobs, or in Ralph Rizzo's case, to his police beat, the women would straighten up the house, do whatever chores the schedule called for, and then, weather permitting, come out to the street with the children. If it was too cold or raining, they would gossip over coffee in the kitchens.

At nights and on weekends the families would gather to share wine, cheese, coffee, and desserts. Then there were always the block parties, Columbus Day celebrations, weddings, and funerals.

"We were one big happy family," recalls Mrs. Edward F. Lawson, a good friend of the Rizzos who lived on South Rosewood but has since moved away. "The times were tough —nobody had any money to speak of—so we all helped each other. The people on Rosewood Street were hard-working, good-living people."

Mrs. Lawson was a close friend of Teresa Rizzo. The two women spent many hours together, drinking coffee and swapping neighborhood gossip.

"I have beautiful memories of those years," she said. "I cried for three months when I moved away."

She went on to describe Teresa Rizzo as a friendly, generous woman.

"She had a heart as big as her body and Francis is the picture of her. She's the kind of woman who would shake hands with one hand and put the coffee pot on with the other. Her house was always open to visitors and the table was usually set for dinner guests. Mrs. Rizzo was a little warmer than the father. But she never let the boys get away with anything."

It was the close camaraderie of the families on South Rosewood Street and Ralph Rizzo's loyalty to his neighbors that almost cost him his job as a policeman.

An inspector in Rizzo's district got a tip one day that a bootlegger who lived on South Rosewood Street was selling illegal whisky out of his row house. The inspector called in Ralph Rizzo and told him of his plan to capture the man red-handed.

The inspector knew that a raid through the front door would give the man time to make adjustments so that the most he could be charged with would be possession. And there weren't many Philadelphians who, despite Prohibition, didn't possess some kind of alcoholic beverage. The police had to catch him in the act of bootlegging and the way to do that, the inspector reasoned, was to enter the man's house through a back window via the roof. A fine plan, the inspector thought, and Ralph Rizzo agreed. Except for one flaw. The inspector wanted to gain access to the roof through Ralph Rizzo's house.

"If you want to get him selling whisky, get him," Ralph told his boss. "But you're not going to use my house to do it. He's my neighbor. How could I ever look him in the face? I have to pass him every day."

The inspector was livid at this display of insubordination. But Ralph Rizzo kept his badge in spite of it and he also kept his honor on South Rosewood Street.*

Respect and honor. They are mentioned frequently when Frank Rizzo talks about himself or his family. They were

* *Philadelphia Magazine*, March 1971.

drilled into him by his father and illustrated by the example the man set for his wife and sons.

"My father was definitely the most important influence on my life," Frank Rizzo said during an interview just after he announced his candidacy for mayor. "If he promised you something, you got it. Dad was a man of high principle. If you asked him for five dollars to go to Atlantic City, he'd tell you to pour salt into the bathtub and climb in. But if you asked for five hundred dollars to repair a leaky roof or do something else for the family, there'd be no questions asked. You got it."

Joseph, one of Frank Rizzo's younger brothers, echoed the same sentiments.

"My father was a very strict man. He wanted us boys to grow up the way he wanted it. He had his own code and was very strict. I feel that was good. I had a lot of respect for my dad. He had high principles. He had his own way of doing things, and you didn't turn him around. We had a lot of respect for policemen when we were kids. We knew they would always be around to handle things. Around the neighborhood we got to know who they were. One thing about my parents in those days: if a neighbor came down to the house and complained that we were doing something wrong, that was it. There wasn't any trial or anything like that. You were wrong. My father would say, 'All right, I'll take care of it.' Then we'd get it with a strap. Sometimes we didn't deserve it, but most of the time we felt we did."

In June 1970, NBC Television aired a report on Rizzo and the Philadelphia Police Department on its *First Tuesday* show. Speaking about the challenge a policeman faces in urban America, Rizzo lapsed into this soliloquy:

"Democracy? What are the values here? What are we giving up? We're giving up rights that belong to us. We've shown too much compassion; we've disregarded the values and feelings of other people who live within the law. I re-

Up from Little Italy || 2 9

member as a young man, there was no question as to who was right or wrong. There were no . . . none of the Democratic formulas applied. My dad set tough rules . . . and you played the game by his rules or you didn't play. There was no free, cut open form, you know . . . boom, you got knocked down, you know, and, uh, good system."

Rizzo today stands six feet two inches tall, and weighs about two hundred fifty pounds. He is barrel-chested with broad shoulders, has a bigger stomach than he ever thought possible, and large hands with thick fingers. He was large for his age even as a boy and a young man, but then he was well proportioned.

As a young boy on South Rosewood Street, Frank Rizzo earned the reputation of being a tough street-fighter. He complemented his size and physical prowess with the same traits of cockiness, self-confidence, and cemented convictions he exhibits so clearly now.

"Frank detested bullies," Joseph Rizzo remembers. "He always went for the underdog. If there was a bully around, Frank would usually go out and find him and take him on. He'd usually come out on top, too. He had many a battle, but in those days it was just with fists, never with guns or knives."

Mrs. Lawson put it this way: "Francis was always a spunky little fellow. He was a tough kid, but he minded his parents."

Mrs. Lawson is particularly fond of Frank Rizzo because he once saved her son from being mauled by a large dog.

"I remember one day my son, who was younger and smaller than Francis, was going down Rosewood Street on his skates. There was a large chow dog in the neighborhood that was very mean. When he saw my son, he started after the boy, but Francis got there first. He picked up the boy, swung him around, and kicked the dog. Believe me, that dog left with his tail tucked between his legs."

Given the nature of Philadelphia's social structure—the domination of the financial and business institutions by the white Anglo-Saxon Protestant elite, its strong Quaker ties, its shameful persecution of the Irish in the mid-1800s, and its discrimination against minority groups—it is surprising that the Italians managed to weave themselves into the fabric of the city's institutions as thoroughly as they did.

For the most part, they immigrated to America as craftsmen and laborers. They chiseled stone, laid bricks, carried hod, tailored clothes, made shoes, cut hair—they were men who worked with their hands. For every one of them who raised himself out of the construction pits and who escaped the sweatshops, there were hundreds bound hopelessly to the blue-collar echelon of low income. It was a fact of life in Philadelphia more than in most major cities that a kid whose last name ended in a vowel came just short of being socially and economically paralyzed at birth.

One alternative to the lunch pail and bent back was the small business; many Italians opened lunch counters, flower shops, delicatessens, grocery stores, fruit markets, or peddled vegetables on the streets. Beyond that was the fast buck, the hustle, the speakeasy, or the numbers racket. And for a minuscule percentage, there was organized crime.

The Italians were no more prone to criminality than other nationalities. In *The Life and World of Al Capone*,* John Kobler cites statistics compiled by the New York City school system in 1910 showing that while Italians made up approximately 11 per cent of the total foreign-born population, only 7 per cent of the foreign-born convicts and juvenile delinquents were Italian.

"Nine years later a federal study covering seventeen nationalities in prisons placed the Italians twelfth in the ratio of commitments per 100,000," Kobler wrote.

* New York: G. P. Putnam, 1971.

But out of the disenchantment with a system that seemed to have no compassion or place for the impoverished ethnic minorities, there grew a generation of the most violent and successful criminals the nation has ever known.

They came snorting out of the Victorian-era ghetto and burst upon the 1920s on the Volstead Act prohibiting the manufacture, sale, and use of alcoholic beverages. They weren't all Italian, to be sure. George "Bugs" Moran, Dion O'Banion, Tommy McErlane, Dutch Schultz, the O'Donnell Brothers, and many other non-Italians played a large part in the crime and corruption of the 1920s and 1930s. Italians were generally the most successful at organizing crime, however, because they used their clannishness and secret societies such as the Black Hand and the Mafia to elevate crime from a street-corner operation to a nationwide syndicate. They infiltrated politics, the police, and the courts, and in Chicago operated with legal impunity.

Organized crime in Philadelphia never rose to the heights that it reached in New York and Chicago. Local hoodlums never dominated the city's government as Al Capone had done in Chicago under Mayor William Hale "Big Bill" Thompson. But while it might have been on less grand a scale in the "City of Brotherly Love," it was just as violent in its approach, just as scornful of legal authority, and just as blatant in its operations.

During Frank Rizzo's boyhood years in South Philadelphia, the Lanzettis, a family of mobsters, the most notorious in the city's history, rose to power in Little Italy. He remembers them well because the name "Lanzetti" was usually spoken in whispers, and that family's exploits were continually being splashed across the front pages of the newspapers. It seemed that almost every day police would find the body of a gangster sprawled in a South Philadelphia gutter or stuffed into one of the boxcars on Washington Street. The Lanzettis were usually blamed. But most of all Frank Rizzo remembers the Lanzettis because he witnessed the fatal shots that brought about their downfall.

Five of the six Lanzetti brothers—Leo, Pius, Lucien, Teo (Theodore), and Ignatius—had been named after popes, their deeply religious mother hoping they would become saints, or at least priests. The youngest was Willie.

They had been raised in a loving home on Catherine Street between 10th and 11th Streets, about a block from the 9th Street open-air market. Their father, a sculptor, had many influential friends and wanted nothing more than for his sons to achieve respectability through honest enterprise. Papa Lanzetti eventually opened the Hotel Taft at 7th and Christian Streets but died shortly thereafter. The family fell on hard times, moved to West Philadelphia, and despite Mama Angelina lighting candles in church every day for her six sons, the street corner, with all its trappings, became their recreation room.

Philadelphia was a very wet town in the 1920s, thanks to the underground booze network established by the "Mustache Petes," the older Mafia men, and some enterprising gang leaders such as Max "Boo Boo" Hoff and Harry "Nig" Rosen.

Because bootlegging and booze-making were the affair of the established mobsters, the Lanzettis, under elder brother Leo's leadership, made their debut into the underworld around 1921 by linking up with a dope-pushing ring in South Philadelphia. Later they moved into the crown and seal supply business, then into white slaving and, after building up these organizations, into commercial racketeering and numbers writing. By 1925 they were in command of much of South Philadelphia's underworld activity.

Such vertical mobility, however, is not accomplished without paying a price. Between August 19 and August 22, in what appeared to be a Lanzetti-initiated gang war, three men died. The first, Joseph Bruno, twenty-six, was shot fourteen times near his home at Catherine Street near 8th Street. This was followed by a near hit on Ignatius the next day. But shortly before 8 p.m. on the twenty-second, the avengers took better aim at the Lanzetti leader. Leo had gone to a bar on 7th Street between Bainbridge and Fitzwater Streets. As he and his brother Lucien downed a drink and prepared to leave, a black sedan drove east on Bainbridge Street and came to a stop at the northeast corner of 7th. Five men, all masked, climbed out and walked over to the southeast corner. Leo and Lucien stepped outside the bar and got two or three steps from the doorway. The five men each fired once, then leaped back into the car and sped away. Leo had been hit twice in the head, twice in the right side, and once in the neck. Lucien was unscathed.

The next night, the body of twenty-eight-year-old Steven Kendig of the Gold Coast gang of Columbia Avenue in North Philadelphia was found on a lonely road in Bucks County, north of the city. He had been shot in the back of the head three times while riding in a car.

Following a modest gangland funeral for Leo, Pius, the next eldest brother, picked up the reins. He moved the family out of Little Italy for about two years while he reorganized its operations and then came back, stronger than before, to face the Mafia and Police Inspector John ("It's me or the Lanzettis in South Philadelphia") Driscoll.

Over the next few years, the Lanzettis were arrested more than fifty times. When they weren't in jail or court, they were dodging Driscoll and his men. There were shootouts with police, and scores of dead bodies were left in the wake of their battles with opposing gangs. In spite of it all, by 1936, Pius had succeeded in dividing up South Philadelphia with Mafia strongman John "Big Nose" Avena.

According to former Police Commissioner Thomas J. Gibbons, Pius fell out with Avena because the latter refused to lend him $18,000 bail money to get Ignatius Lanzetti out of jail in Cape May County, New Jersey. Avena's perfidious attitude plus Pius's growing suspicion that the Mafiosi were cutting into the Lanzettis' numbers bank, set the stage for both their assassination and the demise of the Lanzetti gang.*

Police have never been able to say with moral certainty that Pius put out the order to have Avena killed. But from all the information gathered, from piecemeal testimony, and from those knowledgeable on how organized crime operated in Philadelphia, police have logged this official version:

On August 17, 1936, Avena went to a restaurant at Washington Street and Passyunk Avenue in South Philadelphia to attend a meeting of Philadelphia underworld figures. Presumably, the meeting was called to discuss what to do about the Lanzettis. It was a hot, sticky night and Avena paused outside the restaurant with Martin Feldstein, a member of the Harry "Nig" Rosen gang.

A black sedan, its window curtains pulled down, slowed to a crawl in front of the restaurant. Two sawed-off shotguns were pushed through the drawn curtains and bystanders began to dive into doorways and under parked cars. Avena and Feldstein saw the car too late. They were both killed instantly.

Pius fled town ostensibly to avoid arrest, but police theorize he went to New York to clear himself with Avena's Mafia kin. He returned several months later to take charge of the gang, apparently convinced that no reprisals would be forthcoming.

At 3:50 p.m. on New Year's Eve that year, Pius went to a small lunchroom on Fitzwater Street between 7th and 8th Streets. He ordered a soda pop in the little luncheonette owned by Joseph Gianni, a legendary South Philadelphia boxer who had fought under the name "Joe Grimm." Two other men were in the store at the time, Samuel "Yellow" Roberts, forty-seven, a gambler and pimp who worked for a mortician, and Fortunato Starzi, fifty-seven, a crippled bystander. Joe

* *Philadelphia Daily News*, February 17, 1955.

Grimm was in the basement of his establishment stoking the furnace; his wife, Carrie, waited on the three customers.

Across the street at his grandmother Erminio's house, six-teen-year-old Frank Rizzo was shooting marbles. He noticed a black sedan pull up to a stop in front of the little store and stared inquisitively as three men got out of the car and rushed toward the door of the luncheonette. Pius, nattily dressed as usual, stood at the counter drinking the soda pop. Starzi and Roberts were in a nearby booth. As the men burst through the door, one of them hauled a sawed-off shotgun from under his long, heavy overcoat. The other two men drew revolvers. They blasted Pius to the floor and then turned their guns on the booth. Roberts died instantly; Starzi was rushed to a hospital where he succumbed the next day.

Frank Rizzo, like most residents of the neighborhood, heard the shots. As heads began popping out of windows up and down the street, the three men ran out of the sandwich shop, quickly piled into the car, and fled. Grandmother Erminio ran out of the house, grabbed Frank by the hand, and ordered him inside.

"You didn't see nothing, Frankie," she said excitedly. "You didn't see nothing."

He had, however, seen all but the fatal shots themselves, the shots that brought about the downfall of the Lanzettis. Ignatius served two years of his five-year sentence and then went to Detroit to live with his mother. Teo drew a three-year sentence for transporting narcotics across state lines, and Lucien, after hiding out for a spell, also made his way to Detroit. Only Willie decided to stick it out in Philadelphia. On July 2, 1939, he was found with his head sewed up in a burlap bag, a small-caliber bullet lodged in his brain. He had been dumped behind the stone fence of a Wynnewood estate.

The assassination of Pius Lanzetti was one of the things that led Ralph and Teresa Rizzo to the decision that Little

Italy, despite its ethnic appeal and their strong ties to it, was not the environment in which to raise their four sons. They began saving for a down payment on a home in the Mount Airy section of Philadelphia, a white middle- and upper-class neighborhood in the northern part of the city just above historic Germantown and south of swanky Chestnut Hill.

Frank Rizzo attended elementary classes at the old Matthias W. Baldwin Public School at 16th and Porter Streets, a building that has since been razed. He made average grades and might have done better had he been so motivated. But he was not concerned with scholastics and, for that matter, still isn't. He did his homework because his mother and father saw to it, and he always managed to pass his subjects.

As a young boy, Rizzo set a goal for himself—to be a cop. In this he was encouraged by his father, who had realized the security he had been seeking and the benefits of a regular paycheck. Indeed, Ralph Rizzo wanted all four of his sons to be policemen, a platoon of Rizzos in blue holding steady jobs with the government and the respect of the citizenry. In those days, despite the corruption within the department— the shakedowns and the political influence—Ralph Rizzo knew that policemen were respected, or at least feared. In either case, being a cop meant being "somebody" and Ralph Rizzo passed the message along to his sons many times.

One of the things that kept Frank Rizzo out of trouble in his early days was hard work.

"Frank had some friends down at the corner when we lived on Rosewood Street," said his brother Joseph. "But he never belonged to a gang. Frank wasn't one to hang around."

His first work was shoveling snow and doing odd jobs for his neighbors on South Rosewood Street. A few years later, he got a job as a delivery boy for an American Hardware Store and then became an apprentice meat-cutter in a neighborhood butcher shop.

Frank's father, too, was doing extra work. During his off-duty hours, there were little matters such as taking people to vote or to City Hall to pay their tax bills, or trying to help them straighten out some other legal matter. This was a part of a policeman's job in those days because the department was run by ward leaders and committeemen.

The ward leader usually had a say in the appointment of a precinct captain who, in turn, could pick the men to work under him—men who would perform the services that were needed to keep the politicians in office or assure them of getting their kickbacks and payoffs. Those policemen who refused to cooperate or at least look the other way were transferred. For their cooperation, the captains, the lieutenants, and the sergeants were amply rewarded with money or promise of promotion. A beat patrolman might see an unsolicited coal truck pull up to his house and fill the bin in his basement.

There were honest cops who didn't close their eyes and open their hands. Even they, however, had to perform the political duties that went with being a policeman. Unless a cop was willing to play politics and go on the take, it was difficult to be promoted. Just being a good cop wasn't enough, which helps explain why Ralph Rizzo—an affable, conscientious policeman—never rose beyond the rank of patrolman, although he was on the force for forty-one years.

Ralph Rizzo had joined the Police and Firemen's Band as a clarinetist and was content to collect his paycheck, put in a good day's work, perform whatever "additional" assignments he had to, and then come home. He stayed out of trouble and out of the limelight, preferring the companionship of his wife and boys to tenuous relationships with politicians and ambitious cops.

His son, Frank, on the other hand, was growing restless by the time he was old enough to drive a car. He had completed the Baldwin School, had been graduated from Vare Junior

High School, and by the time he was a senior at Southern High School (now known as South Philadelphia High School), was anxious to see what the world was like outside Little Italy.

While a junior in high school in 1937, Rizzo had joined the Naval Reserve. Midway through his senior year, he dropped out of school and joined the Regular Navy. After basic training at Great Lakes, Rizzo was assigned to the USS *Houston*, a cruiser. He served until November 1939, when he was discharged for medical reasons.*

Upon his discharge, Rizzo came back to South Philadelphia and worked briefly at a construction job. Later he got work at the Midvale Steel Corporation. Meanwhile, the Rizzo family—having saved enough money for a down payment on a home on Mount Pleasant Avenue in Mount Airy— had packed up for the long-awaited move to the northern part of the city. Just before they were to leave, however, Teresa Rizzo was hospitalized with a gall-bladder ailment and, following surgery, died. She was still in her thirties, and

* Rizzo's official biography compiled by the Office of the City Representative contains no mention of his service record, or even the fact that he served at all, although it was no secret that Rizzo had been in the Navy. When he was appointed police commissioner, in May 1967, the city's three newspapers all carried detailed feature stories on him and they noted, without going into detail, that Rizzo was a Navy veteran.

In March 1971, shortly after Rizzo announced his candidacy for the Democratic primary, reporters from both the *Daily News* and the *Inquirer* came up with information concerning his service record.

In 1969, Rizzo, already anticipating his mayoral candidacy, wrote the Department of the Navy requesting that his service record be treated as classified information. He was obliged in his request, and his records were removed from St. Louis, Missouri, and stored in the Pentagon in a special file for "prominent persons."

The records revealed that Rizzo had been discharged honorably. He had contracted a rare disease known as *diabetes insipidus*, an illness Rizzo insists no longer bothers him.

While most men might see this as an unavoidable natural ailment, to Rizzo it was a weakness, a flaw in his constitution. Rizzo deals in absolutes. A man is either strong or weak—a "phony faker" or a member of his "team." There is no middle ground, and Rizzo feared that knowledge of his service record would lead people to believe that he was something less than the toughest cop who ever lived.

her death cast a pall over the Rizzo family and their friends on South Rosewood Street. After the funeral, Ralph Rizzo and his sons moved to 1021 East Mount Pleasant Street. Ralph lived there, amid souvenirs and memories, until he died in April 1968.

In 1943, Frank Rizzo married Carmella M. Silvestri, a girl he had been dating since his discharge from the Navy. Now, as his father had done more than twenty years before, Frank began thinking of security, the future, and the ambitions he had been harboring since he was seven years old. On October 6, 1943, just two weeks short of his twenty-third birthday, Francis Lazzaro Rizzo was sworn in as a patrolman in the Philadelphia Police Department. Ralph Rizzo was extremely pleased. He offered his son congratulations and the following instructions: "Do a good job and stay out of trouble."

The latter advice was incompatible with Rizzo's ambition and ego.

III

"... *He Had This Whimsical Way of Just Clobbering You*"

The man had been arraigned before the judge on a charge of armed robbery and had pleaded not guilty. His trial was set for the next day, and as he was unable to post bond, he was taken back to jail. There it would be the duty of the police to extract a confession.

Just before the suspect was brought into an interrogation room, a captain had rounded up several patrolmen, given them some painters' clothes, brushes, and paint, and had instructed them to give the district headquarters a face-lifting.

As the two policemen painted the ceiling, the suspect was seated in a chair and was given a thorough beating with tightly rolled newspapers—instruments that delivered a good deal of pain but left no marks.

The next day, the man came before the judge and produced a signed confession admitting to the holdup.

"I don't understand," the surprised judge said. "Yesterday you pleaded innocent. Today you have a signed confession."

"Well, Judge," the man replied, "I could take a beating by policemen. But when I saw the painters coming down off their ladders to relieve the police, I gave up."

THE PHILADELPHIA POLICE DEPARTMENT was something less than a shining example of a municipal law-enforcement agency when Frank Rizzo joined it. To begin with, the city had been under the control of the Republican Party since 1895.

Catering to the interests of the downtown business community, real-estate developers, and financial institutions, the old GOP machine usually functioned well politically. But it did little to meet the pressing needs brought on by the social and economic changes that swept the American scene during its time in power.

By the time the Democrats ousted the Republicans in 1951—when Joseph S. Clark and Richardson Dilworth were elected mayor and district attorney, respectively—the city was on the verge of collapse. The center-city business district was in a state of physical deterioration. Rotting hulks of rat-infested buildings occupied entire downtown blocks, and the population of the area had declined from about 75,000 at the turn of the century to about 15,000 at the onset of World War II. The "Chinese Wall," elevated tracks of the Pennsylvania Railroad that were built upon a huge stone foundation, ran from the 30th Street Station down Market Street to 15th Street, near City Hall. The "Wall" divided the area into two districts—one a relatively prosperous business and residential community, the other occupied by factories and warehouses.

Practically no attempt had been made to ease the plight of urban poor, teeming masses of blacks, and other ethnic minorities who lived in cramped row houses throughout the city. The mass-transit system was a shambles and the public schools, under the private domain of Add B. Anderson, the school board's business manager, were hopelessly outmoded in both curriculum and physical facilities, with virtually no new construction having been undertaken in almost three decades.

The charges of political corruption had been so rampant that when William S. Vare, political boss of South Philadelphia, was elected to the United States Senate in 1926, he was denied his seat.

Warner saw these shortcomings as the failing of "privatism," where both the strengths and weaknesses of productivity and social order flowed from private institutions and individual adjustments.

"Privatism left the metropolis helpless to guarantee its citizens a satisfactory standard of living. Privatism encouraged the building of vast new sections of the city in a manner well below contemporary standards of good layout and construction. Privatism suffered and abetted a system of politics which was so weak it could not deal effectively with the economic, physical and social events that determined the quality of life within the city."*

An integral part of any corrupt and neglectful government must be its police department. Philadelphia's department was corrupt in 1943, and there are few policemen who were on the force during those years, including Frank Rizzo, who won't admit it. Indeed, Rizzo proudly looks back on the way he ran the department as compared to the way it operated when he was coming up through the ranks.

"I wouldn't let the politicians have their way," he said. "When I was a patrolman, the bastards had their hands in everything. It was crooked and corrupt. But I changed all that. I ran the department my way."

Those who knew Frank Rizzo say that his personality changed drastically the first time he put on a police uniform. The once restless, tough, but good-natured kid suddenly

* Warner, *op. cit.*, p. 202.

"*. . . He Had This Whimsical Way . . .*" || 43

became a zealous cop. He took his new occupation more as a way of life than a job, and he went after violators of the law like a man possessed.

It is surprising that he ever got out of South Philadelphia, one of his early assignments, because the first car he ticketed for a parking violation belonged to his father's sergeant. Residents of Little Italy—people who had come to expect lenient treatment for minor infractions, particularly if the cop was a fellow Italian—suddenly found themselves getting tickets signed "Patrolman Rizzo."

The complaints began pouring in to his father.

"For a long time," said Ralph Rizzo, "they'd say who is that guy? Then the word got around it was Ralph the Calabrese's son. They didn't understand. But Frank didn't care. If they was wrong, he caught up with them. That's not the way in the neighborhoods—a lot of things, you know, little things, you overlook and maybe you try to just work it out."*

Rizzo began to attract attention as a policeman almost immediately, if not by actions, at least by his vesture. Then, as now, Rizzo prided himself on his personal appearance. As a patrolman on the beat, he was always the image of the spit-and-polish cop. He was well proportioned, tall, and boyishly handsome, with rounded features; he was nothing less than a standout in uniform.

There are cops who operate like refrigerators—men who automatically turn it off when the door to the station closes behind them at the end of their shifts. Rizzo was not one of them. He lived his work.

Most of Rizzo's former superiors, even his counterparts in other cities, are classified by him as "phony fakers." This is his way of saying that no cop was ever so tough or efficient as Rizzo himself. He fondly attributes this to his personal dedication to duty, his self-styled crusade against criminals

* *Philadelphia Magazine*, July 1967.

and those who would question or flout the law. Even as a rookie patrolman, he exhibited these characteristics, and they were not lost on his superiors and the media.

Rizzo first hit the newspapers in 1944, when he was burned trying to extinguish an awning fire at Tulpehocken and Baynton Streets. It was a brief mention, but enough to prompt newspaper librarians to open a file titled RIZZO, FRANK L.; the file is now measured by the pound.

Rizzo made the newspapers again in 1948, when he was on duty as a patrolman at Broad Street and Erie Avenue in North Philadelphia. Responding to a call that five men were in the process of robbing a taxi driver, he arrived at the scene as the men were roughing up the cabbie, and he waded into the middle of it. The five men made the mistake of resisting Rizzo's efforts to arrest them. After a brief scuffle, four were taken to the hospital while the fifth, like Rizzo, suffered some bad bruises. The elements of physical violence and the suppression of force with superior force evidenced here were to become Rizzo trademarks.

"There were two ways to be arrested by Rizzo," a former associate said. "The easy way or the hard way. It didn't make any difference to him. If a guy wanted to come along quietly, all right. If he got smart or wanted to play rough, well, Frank liked that, too."

Put another way, Rizzo was renowned for placing a few well-aimed fists in a man's stomach or rib cage, where the effects would go unnoticed by a judge. He also swung a good nightstick, but that was reserved for those who dared resist arrest. And there were many.

Rizzo was directing traffic at the corner of Broad Street and Erie Avenue one morning when Judge Samuel H. Rosenberg, then Director of Public Safety, noticed him. Rosenberg was particularly impressed by Rizzo's ramrod posture and his impeccable attire.

"Who's that cop?" he asked a man riding with him.

"That's Ralph Rizzo's son," the man replied.

Rosenberg knew Ralph Rizzo through the latter's membership in the Police and Firemen's Band, which was on call at the beckoning of politicians, judges, and other local officials.

Rosenberg, despite protests from Republican ward leaders, made the young patrolman an acting sergeant. He was assigned to the 33rd District in South Philadelphia, with instructions to break up a flourishing gambling operation in the 7th and Carpenter Streets area. Ironically, one of the men assigned to his platoon was Ralph Rizzo.

"The first couple of times I tried raiding this one particular numbers joint, I used the usual procedure," Frank said. "I'd tell the lieutenant where we were going and get my men and move. By the time we'd get there the place would be empty. So I finally figured out that the lieutenant and my own men were protecting the operation. The next time I went by myself and hauled the whole goddamned bunch of them in. Well, you should have seen it when we went to court. They had six or seven lawyers and everyone was dressed up in silk suits. Christ, the judge stood up when they came into the courtroom. They got off with a small fine. But I fixed their asses the next time. I busted in the door, called for a wagon, and had them taken away. Then I went upstairs and threw their adding machines out the window. I knew I couldn't get them fined very much, but the machines were worth at least a hundred dollars. It wasn't long before they were out of business."

Ralph Rizzo was awed by his son's disregard of the political shock waves he was causing. Frank remembers one conversation they had:

"Take it easy, Franny, you're ruining my name," said his father.

"Don't worry, Pop, this is a different time. Things aren't going to be like they used to be."

Rizzo says he had to have his father transferred to avoid further embarrassments and family squabbles.

"I couldn't have him working for me. It didn't look right."

By 1951, Rizzo had made connections with many of South Philadelphia's political powers, including Frank Palumbo, the night-club owner and restaurateur—a man known for being able to deliver votes. And 1951 also was the year that Rizzo took his civil-service test to be promoted to sergeant. He passed it on November 18, and Rosenberg, who has since been made a judge, conveniently had the list of the remaining 599 candidates thrown out. He said it was "outdated."*

"You should have heard the bastards [politicians] scream," Rizzo said laughingly. "Sure it was political. But I was the best damn cop they had and they knew it."

Sergeant Rizzo's first assignment was to the Motor and Highway Patrol in the 33rd District at 7th and Carpenter Streets, where, in the course of the next year and a half, he earned himself a nickname that has become the stuff of Philadelphia legend—the "Cisco Kid."

Some insiders say that Rizzo picked up that tag by wearing two pearl-handled pistols. That would seem to fit the image, but Rizzo insists he has never owned a pearl-handled gun. Others say it was a matter of timing—that his hard-charging raids on illegal gambling operations came at a time when the "Cisco Kid" was a popular television cowboy.

But Rizzo's version of the story is quite different. It all happened, the former commissioner says, when he answered a call about a shooting on Montrose near 4th and Christian Streets in South Philadelphia. A gunman had fired several shots as police cars began streaming in. Rizzo was the first man on the scene and he quickly barked orders to his men while taking off on foot after the fleeing suspect.

A small boy, seeing Rizzo personally take up the chase,

* *Evening Bulletin*, January 4, 1972.

began yelling, "The Cisco Kid'll get him! The Cisco Kid'll get him!" Rizzo got the man. He also got the nickname, and it stuck.

On January 16, 1952, Rizzo was made acting captain of the 16th Police District, headquartered at 39th Street and Lancaster Avenue in West Philadelphia.

Rizzo said shortly after taking over the post that the area, predominantly black, had the city's highest crime rate and that the trouble stemmed from the proliferation of speakeasies. In typical blitzkreig fashion, Rizzo went after the speakeasies and the men who operated them. With sirens screaming and men bursting through doors, Rizzo began compiling an impressive record of arrests in the district. In March 1952, his men logged 657 arrests, and maintained an average of more than 600 a month during the rest of his time there. But his conviction rate was far below the arrest rate—statistics in Rizzo's crime-fighting history that have always been disproportionate. He has blamed at different times everyone but the police for the low conviction rate, never publicly admitting, what is a commonly known fact, that careless and sloppy police work is frequently responsible for cases being thrown out of court and defendants being acquitted.

In this instance, Rizzo blamed lack of citizen cooperation for his inability to close up the speakeasies. In an interview with a neighborhood newspaper in April 1952, Rizzo said: "There are approximately two hundred speakeasies in this district. We get many, many complaints from residents in the vicinity of these bawdyhouses, but from fear of reprisals they refuse to appear in court and substantiate their information after arrests have been made."*

While storeowners and businessmen in the 16th District looked upon Rizzo as a white Messiah come to save them

* *The Neighborhood Advertiser*, April 10, 1952.

from the ravages of hoodlums and stick-up men, the area's civic leaders and many of its citizens were up in arms. There were so many complaints being filed with then District Attorney Richardson Dilworth against Rizzo and his men that Frank Brookhauser, a popular columnist for the *Evening Bulletin*, wrote: "The DA's office just doesn't know what to do with them."

Most of the complaints charged that Rizzo and his men had violated the civil rights of arrested suspects, that they had searched without warrants, used unnecessary physical force, beaten people into signing confessions, and discriminated against blacks—charges that were continuously being filed against Rizzo until he resigned as police commissioner in February 1971.

Undoubtedly, some of the charges were true. Just as surely, Rizzo wasn't always responsible, at least not directly. What was beginning to evolve, however, was a pattern of Rizzo's men attempting to emulate him. If a captain could split open heads or search a house without a warrant or gut-punch a suspect into a confession, what was to stop a sergeant or a patrolman from doing the same things? What better way to impress a superior than to employ his own techniques? The ranks generally reflect the values and thinking of the leadership. Rizzo perpetuated his tough-guy image and he would defend his men under the most questionable of circumstances.

Rizzo repeatedly maintained that he would not fault a mistake in judgment on the part of a policeman, but that he would blanch at a willful violation of a policeman's code of ethics. The problem was that Rizzo's loose interpretation of "mistaken judgment" became a cover-up for the most blatant and unwarranted actions on the part of his men. Once, when he was defending one of his men in court, he shouted at a prosecuting attorney, "Don't get involved with me or you'll be worrying about your own rights."

The effect of all this was tantamount to giving his men

carte blanche in the streets, and they took advantage of the wide latitude time and again.

On May 27, 1952, Rizzo was transferred from the 16th District and was given an assignment that was to gain him almost as much local notoriety as he received later during the years he ran the police department. He took command of the 19th District at 12th and Pine Streets, which included the center-city business district and the Locust Street "strip."

Just two days later, Rizzo was back in the headlines for an early-morning raid he conducted on the old Top Hat Café, 1235 Locust Street, just after the mandatory closing hour of 2 p.m. Rizzo claimed he had seen the bartender serve a patron a drink. Over loud protestations and some shoving, the owner, the bartender, the waitress, and nine patrons were arrested.

All but one of the patrons were released from custody the next morning. He had to pay ten dollars for the repair of a rip in Rizzo's new seventy-dollar suit before the magistrate would let him out of jail.

It was an omen of what was to come in center city during the next seven years. Rizzo would be a one-man show—a spectacle that would delight some, infuriate others, and, thanks to the publicity he received, transform him into a genuine folk hero.

If there is a clear document of Rizzo's intolerance of lifestyles other than his own, it is the chronicle of this period when he conducted his harassing raids on the coffeehouses in center city.

About a half dozen espresso shops had sprung up in the downtown business district during the late 1950s. They went by such intriguing names as The Proscenium, The Artist's Hut, and The Humoresque. The bill of fare in most of them was, of course, coffee. But they supplied the artistic community—both genuine and pseudo—with folk music, imported teas, chess and checker sets, and a place to gather.

They seemed to be operating within the law and did little to attract Rizzo's attention until local residents began complaining that "weirdos" and "homosexuals" were "contaminating" the sedate center-city residential area, causing traffic problems, and "corrupting the morals" of the city.

That was all Captain Rizzo had to hear. Most of the citizen complaints were baseless, but Rizzo went after the coffeehouses as if he were carrying out a holy war against the infidels.

"It was just incredible," said Spencer Coxe, head of the Philadelphia Chapter of the American Civil Liberties Union. "Rizzo would bust in night after night, haul everyone to headquarters, and then they would be released. Most weren't even booked. Only a few were ever found guilty of anything and they were charged with disorderly conduct."

The raids eventually shut down most of the coffeehouses, which clearly had been Rizzo's intent. One of the few to remain in business was The Humoresque, whose owner, Melvin Heifetz, finally asked then United States District Judge Thomas J. Clary to grant an injunction restraining Rizzo from raiding his establishment. Rizzo was promoted and transferred before the judge could render a decision.

Rizzo was not only contemptuous of those he considered "criminals," but openly rebuked those who would defend them or those who would criticize the police.

An example was a shouting match he engaged in on April 24, 1958, with Magistrate M. Philip Freed, who had been holding court in the 12th and Pine Street station house for only twenty-three days, just long enough to have become disgusted at the number of persons arrested whom he could see no grounds for detaining.

One of Rizzo's men, Lieutenant William Baker, was in Freed's court—part of the station house—that day for a hearing involving two men whom he had arrested on a numbers-writing charge.

Freed thought the charge so weak that he told the court, "I'm holding each in three hundred dollars' bail just to show the grand jury the kind of arrests being made in this district in the heart of the city's worst gambling area. Can't these guys bring in anybody important?"

With that, Rizzo came bounding out of his office.

"Faker," he yelled at Freed.

"You're one, too," Freed replied.

"You're a phony," Rizzo persisted.

"And so are you," Freed shot back.

His temper past the boiling point, Rizzo shouted at the top of his voice, "You're a misfit." Then, turning to the court stenographer, added, in an equally loud voice, "And put that in the record."*

It did not seem to matter that those he arrested might be innocent of the charges he placed against them. If they were not living within the boundaries of Rizzo's own moral and ethical code, if they appeared to be in violation of what he considered to be the "right" way to operate a public establishment, he "took them on."

"Look," he said during an interview on August 31, 1971, "it was either me or them. I would haul some of these characters in ten, fifteen times. I knew the charges wouldn't stick. But it was a matter of seeing who would get tired first, me hauling them in or them being hauled in. I had all the time in the world. These bastards didn't. I remember one guy who I knew was involved in the numbers. I told him he couldn't do that in my district. But every day, I'd see him standing on the corner. So I began arresting him. For about twenty-six days, I think, Sundays not included, I pulled him in. One day I got him three times. He finally moved out."

Rizzo's style was anything but subtle. Conscious of the benefits of getting his name in print, he conducted raids in a

* *Philadelphia Daily News*, April 24, 1958.

manner that would draw the attention of the press. He would answer a call with ten policemen when one would have easily sufficed. He blared the sirens when a quiet knock on a door would have accomplished the same results. He would haul people to jail when a reprimand would do.

On October 1, 1958, painter-illustrator Emlen Etting held a party in honor of Josh Logan, the director of *The World of Suzie Wong*, which was playing in Philadelphia at the time. Etting's apartment was located at 1922 Panama Street, a quaint, narrow street that had been rebuilt along its original lines as part of the effort to restore the old downtown area. Among the twenty-five guests were France Nuyen, star of the show, who also had played the part of Polynesian beauty Liat in the movie version of *South Pacific*, and actress Kay Medford, as well as other members of the cast.

One of Etting's neighbors complained about the noise coming from the apartment. Two policemen arrived and, according to Etting, "quite politely" told him to keep the noise down. Etting said he obliged. About an hour later, however, three squad cars pulled up in front of his apartment in the narrow street.

Rizzo banged on the door and told Etting, "Unless you and your goddamned pansy friends get back in the house, quiet down, and shut up, I will throw you all in the paddy wagon and throw you in with the drunks for the night."

Rather than have his guests spend the night in the 12th and Pine Streets station house, Etting moved the party to a friend's house around the corner. But by this time there was considerable yelling and the police were doing most of it, he said. Neighbors were awakened and soon the street took on the appearance of a block party.

Etting filed an official complaint with Mayor Dilworth charging that the police were "loud, rude, and behaved like Cossacks." Dilworth sent the complaint along to Police Commissioner Thomas J. Gibbons. The matter was dropped.

Pennsylvania liquor laws are so complex and picayune that on any given night, almost every bar in the state can be shut down for one or more violations. The Liquor Control Board recognizes this, and for the most part, so do the police. Usually only the most blatant violations of the liquor laws are prosecuted. And even these can be avoided if the owner is prepared to pay the cost. A man who used to own a taproom near the Police Administration Building, known as the Roundhouse, explained why eventually he had to change addresses.

"I got tired of paying for protection," he said. "At Christmas, every cop in the district would come by for his present. Ten dollars a clip. It'd cost me two or three hundred dollars just to keep the doors open. Other times, it would be for the death of a cop, or a promotion, or transfer. Hell, man, I was running a straight operation. Can you imagine what it would have been if I had been making numbers or horse bets?"

Captain Rizzo would use the most obscure regulations to shut down operations he found personally offensive. His favorite targets were those that even hinted at sexual permissiveness. Lou's Moravian Bar, at 1507 Moravian Street in center city, featured a "Continuous Strip Tease Battle," with one girl grinding at a bar downstairs, another upstairs. Rizzo, on a Friday night in 1958, hit Lou's Moravian like a thunderbolt. He arrested the dancers, the owner's son, Sidney Mass, three Drexel Institute students who were there to get autographs of the dancers as part of their fraternity initiation, and the owner, Joseph C. Mass.

At a stormy hearing the next day in the 12th and Pine Street station house, young Mass hung yet another moniker on Rizzo.

"This man is the Nero of the night-club belt," he shouted at the magistrate.

Rizzo yelled back, "You're operating a dive—the worst I've ever seen in the central-city area."

Rizzo then told the magistrate that he had raided the place because of the strip-tease shows.

"It wasn't their lack of clothing we minded so much," he said. "It was their gyrations."

That same night he shut down the Allegro Bar at Spruce near Broad Street, hauling in the patrons, bartender, waitresses, and owner, and succeeded in getting them fined in amounts ranging from $5 to $300.

The hearings in the 12th and Pine Street station house became a show in themselves. Following a Rizzo raid, city editors would send a reporter to cover the hearing. The reporter usually returned to the newsroom with a colorful story.

One spring night in 1954, for example, the "Rizzo Raiders" swooped down on three center-city night spots and arrested seven persons, including four members of a female-impersonating team known as the "Gay Boy Revue" and three shapely strip-tease dancers.

The charges were so weak that even the assistant district attorney assigned to prosecute the case, Stanley Bashman, agreed that the shows being performed by the accused weren't lewd or indecent.

"After all," he said, "evil often is only in the eye of the viewer."

The charges against the seven were dismissed, but not before Rizzo engaged in one of his usual asides.

"I'll raid them again tonight," he shouted. "We'll see who gets tired quicker—of them being brought in here every night or doing away with that type of show."

A defense attorney, Alfred Ginsberg, quickly rose and told Rizzo, "You can't threaten my clients that way. These people have every right to earn a living."

The two men then exchanged more shouts and finally Ginsberg, in sheer frustration, said to Rizzo, "You're my size, I'll take you."

Rizzo would have loved nothing more than to take on the lawyer. But before the two could square off, a policeman shoved the owner of one of the bars onto the ropes in front of the hearing bench, while Magistrate J. Amos Harris furiously rapped his gavel.

"If you officers don't act properly I'll throw you in jail," he threatened.

Rizzo called his men to order and then fired back at the magistrate, "All right, you're the boss in here, but we're the boss on the street."*

While Rizzo's tactics drew sharp criticism from men like Spencer Coxe, the majority of Philadelphians felt he was merely doing what any cop should do. A cop was supposed to be tough. Criminals belonged in jail. So what if he got a little feisty now and then? He was on the job, wasn't he? He was protecting the citizenry. Better Rizzo than a cop asleep in the patrol car. This, by and large, was the response Rizzo read, and because he felt the majority of the people were behind him, he continually attempted to reinforce his image.

But there were complaints and lawsuits charging him with brutality, and there were several investigations held by different agencies (including the police department itself). Complainants, however, have had a difficult time getting their charges to stick. One of the first complaints filed against Rizzo was in August 1955. Its dismissal established a general pattern that still holds.

The complaint had been filed by five Navy hospital corpsmen who alleged that Rizzo and Patrolman Robert O'Brien beat them viciously with a nightstick and then lined them up against the 12th and Pine Street station-house wall and administered another beating. They also claimed that O'Brien had pummeled them with a rubber hose while herding them into a cell.

Rizzo, in his official report of the incident, said he had

* *Philadelphia Daily News*, April 28, 1954.

witnessed a car occupied by the corpsmen and a civilian racing through center-city streets. He also claimed that the occupants hurled insults at a woman and her escort. Rizzo was on foot at the time; he said he and Patrolman Herman Levin commandeered a taxi and caught up with the car.

In the usual stormy hearing at the station house, Rizzo admitted under oath that he had resorted "to some force" in arresting the corpsmen after they shoved him around.

The taxi driver substantiated a portion of Rizzo's testimony. He said he ran after his taxi and arrived at the scene of the brawl a few minutes later, only to be elbowed in the mouth so hard that he had to have a tooth pulled.

The corpsmen and the civilian denied they had been unruly once they were stopped, alleging that the fight broke out after Rizzo began beating them with his nightstick.

Following frequent spontaneous outbursts at the hearing, which lasted three hours and forty-five minutes, Magistrate E. David Keiser dismissed the charges against Rizzo and O'Brien, saying, "Nothing can be gained by going into court with all this hysteria. The ends of justice will best be served if the police, City Solicitor, and District Attorney become fully acquainted with the facts contained in testimony. A better understanding can be reached through a conference of naval authorities and city officials."*

Rizzo was later cleared of all charges, due in no small part to the fact that one of his attorneys was the late State Senator Benjamin J. Donolow, a powerful political leader.

One man who followed Rizzo during his stay in center city said: "He inspired fear. When he walked the street a whole wave of fear preceded him. All these little guys, small-time hoods, went scurrying up alleys when they saw him coming. He was a real fist-in-the-belly guy. A cold rage would come over him; he'd go almost blank and then, bang, in the gut. He didn't need the badge or the gun or the stick.

* *Philadelphia Inquirer*, August 26, 1955.

". . . He Had This Whimsical Way . . ." || 5 7

He had damn good fists. Maybe he's changed, but in those days he had this whimsical way of just clobbering you."*

In spite of the questionable nature of many of his raids and arrests, Rizzo did perform numerous acts of public service. He succeeded in bringing to trial notorious gamblers, bootleggers, and Shylocks. He caught muggers, murderers, and robbers where they had operated with near impunity before. Indeed, throughout his stay in center city, there was not a single armed robbery. His official biography shows that he received eighty-nine citations from various civic and social organizations, ranging from a citation from Mayor James H. J. Tate because Philadelphia had the lowest crime rate of the ten largest American cities to the "Arms of the City and Royal Burgh of Edinburgh, Scotland." There also are awards from the Philadelphia Histadrut Council, the Director's Honor Award from the United States Secret Service, a citation from the Pennsylvania House of Representatives for work in the field of narcotics, and from the Crime Commission of Philadelphia.

Among his most cherished honors is the *Philadelphia Inquirer* Hero Award, which he received in February 1953, for possibly having saved the lives of two men.

On his way home from the 12th and Pine Street station, after having been on duty for eighteen hours, Rizzo spotted a group of men attacking two others. As he got out of his car, some of the attackers fled, but three remained and attacked him. After a fierce gun battle, he arrested the three attackers and then summoned aid for the two badly beaten victims. Doctors said that had he not arrived when he did and summoned help, the two men would have died.

There were other times when his fearlessness thrust him into the limelight. One night in November 1953 Rizzo was returning from a meeting of the Spruce Street Area Improve-

* *Philadelphia Magazine*, July 1967.

ment Association at which he had been awarded a plaque for his work as a crime fighter. Still carrying it and dressed in civilian clothes, he came upon a burglary suspect.

Rizzo drew his service revolver, and held the man at bay, hoping that a patrol car making the rounds of the neighborhood would come by. But no sooner had he stopped the suspect than a man with a pistol came running out of a nearby house, yelling, "Drop that gun."

Rizzo kept his revolver pointed at the suspect.

"I'm a police officer . . . call a red car!" he barked.

But the man waved the pistol menacingly and replied, "What did you say? I can't hear you, but you'd better drop that gun."

Rizzo quickly realized that the man was a hard-of-hearing neighborhood resident who had mistaken him for a holdup man. And just as the captain began considering the alternatives, a police car pulled up and solved the problem. It had been summoned by a neighbor who had heard the commotion in the street.

If there were doubts about Rizzo's suitability for high command, they were not shared by the top police brass, or by the politicians. Indeed, Frank Rizzo had already become something of a legend by the time he began harassing the coffeehouses. There were those who hated him—those who thought he represented repression and brutality. But on March 18, 1959, when Rizzo was promoted to inspector and assigned to the Northeast as district commander, most of the city thought the promotion was well deserved.

Stewart Klein of the *Daily News* captured the mood of center city upon the announcement of Rizzo's transfer in this poem, published by the paper on March 29:

> In the night of center-city
>> When the traffic does not roar,
> It is whispered half in pity:
>> "He don't live here anymore."

"*. . . He Had This Whimsical Way . . .*" ‖ 5 9

In the Locust St. coffee parlors,
  Through the doors he often tore,
Say it softly, no one hollers:
  "He don't live here anymore."
Down Mole, Ranstead, Quince,
  The streets of days of yore;
Sly smiles instead of winces:
  "He don't live here anymore."
Somewhere the hoods are crying,
  Somewhere the dips are sore,
But expressoed lips are sighing:
  "He don't live here anymore."

The day he assumed command of the Northeast district, Rizzo hit the front pages of the newspapers by issuing a warning.

"If there is any gambling activity going on, I'm sure it will only be a short time before those who are in back of it know I am here," the *Sunday Bulletin* quoted him as saying. "I don't think I will have any coffee shops in the Northeast that I will be concerned with."

But the suburban Northeast district, mainly white and middle class, was a totally different area from center city and the other urban neighborhoods where Rizzo had cut his police teeth. Commenting on his assignment after working at it for a few months, Rizzo said, "It's like being in another police department. Imagine having corn fields, geese, pheasants, and deer in the jurisdiction."

It was not the place for an ambitious cop to make his mark. Rizzo longed for the back alleys and the hot, crowded streets. That was where the action was. That was where he could get into the thick of it. He didn't have to wait too long for his ticket to leave.

In January 1960, Commissioner Gibbons transferred him to the West Philadelphia Division, with orders Rizzo could hardly have improved upon himself.

"I want West Philadelphia cleaned up and Inspector Rizzo is my clean-up man."

Gibbons had been appointed police commissioner by Democratic Mayor Joseph Clark and had been retained by Clark's successor, Richardson Dilworth. Showing no particular flair for innovation or administration, Gibbons nevertheless fit well into the Clark-Dilworth reformist policy of keeping the department free of politics.

Gibbons' appointments were made on his appraisal of a man's ability. Only those he considered most deserving were promoted, with little deference paid to the time-honored tradition of pleasing the ward heelers and committeemen, which says something about the esteem in which he held Rizzo.

Even Dilworth, despite the protests about Rizzo, respected his gung-ho attitude. A former Marine officer in World War I, Dilworth appreciated toughness. He frequently winced at Rizzo's tactics and lack of subtlety but on the whole considered him to be a good cop at the time.

Gibbons retired in July 1960 and was succeeded by Albert Brown, a soft-spoken, intelligent policeman who had come up through the ranks. But by the time Brown took over the department, reform government had become a part of the city's history. Mayor James H. J. Tate, as City Council president, had automatically become mayor when Dilworth resigned in order to run for governor. Tate was pure politician and he knew that the police department could be used as a political arm of the machine in power.

Meanwhile, Rizzo was making himself felt in his new assignment as commander of the West Philadelphia district, a predominantly black section of the city.

About two weeks after he took over, Rizzo sent one of his men to a private club to see if all was on the up-and-up. When the doors of the club closed at 3 a.m. as state law required, the bar remained opened, a violation. Rizzo's spy bought several illegal drinks and then called his inspector from a pay phone. Within minutes, Rizzo arrived with four other policemen and arrested ten late-drinking patrons and three employees.

The raid was not unlike dozens of others that Rizzo had conducted except that he had taken on the 46th Ward Democratic Club, located on 52nd Street between Locust and Spruce Streets. Local politicians were aghast. But that was Rizzo's way of letting them know that business would not be run as usual.

Rizzo remained in West Philadelphia for less than a year. On August 10, 1960, he returned to the area in which he had gained his fame, the Central Division. Only this time he was an inspector and not a captain and the only man he had to answer to was Commissioner Albert Brown.

That year on Christmas Eve, Frank Rizzo almost lost his life.

A man standing on the corner of Pine and Smedley Streets pointed a .38-caliber revolver at Rizzo from a distance of about fifteen feet and told him not to move.

Rizzo moved forward. The man pulled the trigger but the pistol misfired. Rizzo kept coming, and the man pulled the trigger again. Misfire. Miraculously, the loaded weapon failed to fire a third time before Rizzo pounced on him, fists flailing.

During the early 1960s Rizzo concentrated his efforts on the "Locust Street Strip," a three-block stretch of "bust-out" joints that specialized in B-girls who gouged unwary customers for watered-down drinks and magnums of champagne.

He forced several of them out of business, temporarily at least, and the publicity poured freely in the newspapers and on television and radio. So notorious did the "Rizzo Raiders" become that in June 1962 both Brown and Rizzo were called to Washington to testify before Senator John Mc-

Clellan's subcommittee investigating the works of the American Guild of Variety Artists.

Brown told the committee that "repeated police action" had curbed B-girl activity in Philadelphia, leaving little doubt that "Rizzo's Raiders" were singularly responsible for the cleanup.

Rizzo had thus been thrust upon the national scene, and back in Philadelphia they loved it.

By 1963 more than one high-ranking police official had come to realize that the Clark-Dilworth policy of keeping the department free of political influence had created a potentially more dangerous problem. Into the vacuum created by the absence of meddling hacks came the racketeers. While politicians might try to influence appointments and promotions, while they might use the police to perform extracurricular activities such as taking citizens to register or to vote or to campaign actively for whatever party held sway at the time, they could not afford a scandal. In the absence of political influence, however, racketeers felt perfectly safe in offering bribes to policemen to keep them from the doors of their gambling establishments and speakeasies.

In October the Internal Revenue Service, in a carefully planned raid, swooped down on a numbers operation at 2nd and Christian Streets in South Philadelphia. A subsequent investigation pointed to police collusion with the gamblers. The purge was on.

Howard Regis Leary, a reticent Irishman who had earned a law degree from Temple University by attending night session, had replaced Brown as commissioner.

Following the IRS raid, Leary immediately instituted a complete shake-up in the brass. Inspectors were moved around like so many chessmen and the man he picked to clean up the "hot spot" in South Philadelphia was Frank Rizzo.

Then Leary, a top-flight administrator, began working

with police and government officials in New York, Los Angeles, San Francisco, and Detroit to devise a new organizational scheme for the 7000-man Philadelphia Police Department. He presented it to Mayor Tate, who gave his approval, and on December 12, 1963, City Managing Director Fred T. Corleto called a press conference to announce the plan.

The table of organization at that time had slots for two deputy commissioners, but one of the posts had been vacant. Leary expanded this to four and set the salary at $14,000 a year.

One of the four men named to the new jobs was Frank Rizzo. He was put in charge of all uniformed forces, which gave him virtual control of the department. The old deputy commissioner, Theodore Mitchell, reverted to the rank of inspector and took a corresponding cut in pay.

Edward J. Bell was put in charge of detectives. Bell, forty-one at the time, was a close personal friend of Mayor Tate's. He was frequently referred to as "Tate's cop." John Driscoll, who had replaced Rizzo in the Central Division, was made responsible for the liaison with other law-enforcement agencies. Richard T. Edwards, the first Negro in the department's history to attain the rank of deputy commissioner, was put in charge of community programs.

So it was that in 1964, Francis Lazzaro Rizzo, forty-three, a veteran of twenty years on the force, stood at the threshold of becoming the most dominant personality in Philadelphia.

He had more than 6000 men under his command. And he had already captured the imagination of the city's 2 million citizens. During the next seven years he would convince them that they would never see the likes of him again.

IV

The Making of a Supercop

It was one of those routine calls that crackle across the J-band dozens of times each day.

"Man with a gun . . ."

The location was a third-story apartment in a large building on Erie Avenue, west of Broad Street in North Philadelphia. The patrolman responding to the call screeched to a halt in front of the house, drew his revolver, and ran up the stairs. He was met with a hail of gunfire which he promptly returned. The suspect slumped to the floor mortally wounded.

The officer then ran back to car and radioed a report. Within minutes, police cars, reporters, photographers, an ambulance, and the coroner were at the scene.

Reporters and photographers, clamoring to find out what had happened, were told they couldn't enter the building. They stood by impatiently waiting for the unmarked black Chrysler to arrive. When it did, Frank Rizzo stepped out, quickly ran upstairs, and then passed the word to let the newsmen come up.

"Careful men, careful men," he cautioned as they entered the apartment. "Don't step on him."

There in the kitchen of the apartment near the rear entrance was the naked corpse of a black man, a pool of blood at his side. The coroner's men had stripped him to check for the entry and exit marks of the bullets that had taken his life.

Rizzo seated the newsmen within spitting distance of the body and held a press conference.

"There's one who won't take another shot at a cop," he told reporters.

IF EVER A MAN'S DESTINY was linked to a point in time or to a particular social climate, it was Frank L. Rizzo's in the summer of 1964. Philadelphia, like most of the nation's big cities, was gripped by a fear of violence that was beginning to boil up out of American ghettos. Philadelphians lived with the unsettling thought that at any moment its impoverished black citizens might rise up in destructive riot. They didn't have to wait long.

At 9:30 p.m. on a hot Friday, August 28, a motorcycle patrolman responded to a call that an auto was blocking the intersection of 22nd Street and Columbia Avenue in the black-ghetto area of North Philadelphia. A man and a woman in the car were having a noisy quarrel. Traffic was backing up and onlookers were gathering.

The patrolman pulled up and rushed in to break up the ruckus. When he tried to coax the woman from behind the wheel of the car, however, she began punching and kicking him. Seconds later, a bystander came to the woman's aid and the crowd began closing in. The woman was finally subdued and led to a police wagon. But before police could clear the area, the first salvo of bricks and bottles began sailing from nearby rooftops and doorways. A long weekend of rioting had gotten under way.

Police Commissioner Howard R. Leary had gone to the

South Jersey shore for the weekend. He was reached soon after the rioting erupted. As Leary began speeding the sixty miles eastward, his second in command, Deputy Commissioner Rizzo, had arrived at the scene and began making plans to quell the escalating disturbance.

He called for reinforcements and, after studying the situation, decided on a frontal assault, a charge down Columbia Avenue to sweep the streets of the looters. He would shoot if he had to, arrest when he could. The rioting and looting, he figured, could be quashed in a matter of minutes. But Rizzo was never to find out if his plan would work. In what has become one of the most controversial events in the department's history, Leary pulled up to Columbia Avenue just as his deputy commissioner was ready to deploy his troops and ordered him to pull the men back. Rizzo balked momentarily.

"For the first time in my life I almost refused to obey an order," Rizzo reflected during an interview seven years later. "But I didn't. Leary was my superior and it was my duty to obey him."

Rizzo insists to this day that had he been allowed to use the force he had assembled, in the manner he had intended, the riot would have been short-lived. Mayor Tate agrees.

"If Leary had not backed down, we wouldn't have lost control of the streets," Tate said. "If Rizzo had been in full command throughout the period, we wouldn't have had a riot."

Tate was miffed by the operation because he was one of the last to be informed of what was happening.

"Leary finally contacted me through Zecca [deputy to the mayor, Anthony Zecca] at six in the morning. I finally got hold of Leary and it was 10 a.m. before we could call a cabinet meeting."

Leary, however, had different thoughts about what happened that night. To him the situation was more complex than simply charging down Columbia Avenue. He knew that snipers could be hiding on the roofs and in the upper floors of the buildings that lined both sides of the street. And he didn't think the police were equipped properly (they had no hard hats, for example). Leary concluded that the Columbia Avenue terrain was much like a blind canyon, and he feared that police sweeping down the street would trigger a shooting spree.

Eventually Rizzo got to use his men, but by that time— several hours later—it was no longer a matter of taking control of Columbia Avenue. The riot had spread over a wide area and pockets of smaller disturbances were erupting all over North Philadelphia. As fast as peace was restored to one area, violence sprang up in another. By the time it was all over late Sunday night, an estimated 2000 blacks had participated in the rioting and looting. Several hundred persons, including fifteen policemen, had been injured. Store windows had been smashed, untold amounts of goods had been looted, and property damage was heavy. But not one person had been killed.

Whether Rizzo might have prevented the riot from becoming as large as it did or whether Leary saved the lives of the police, rioters, looters, and bystanders by pulling the police back at a critical time remains an unresolved question. In retrospect, the Columbia Avenue riot was significantly smaller in scale and less violent in nature than those that followed it in other cities across the country.

But two significant developments could be directly related to the events surrounding Columbia Avenue that August night. Any lingering doubts that Rizzo and Leary represented two vastly different approaches to the use of police power had been dispelled. Rizzo would not hesitate to use whatever force was necessary to quell a civil disturbance. And he wasn't overly concerned that blood might be shed. He considered this a calculated risk, one that must be taken.

Leary would use force too, but only when all else failed. He feared for the safety of his men and for the accused, preferring to exploit the subtleties of power rather than its awesome strength. Given a choice between possible bloodshed and certain property damage, Leary would opt for the latter.

This disagreement went beyond the mere question of how and under what circumstances and conditions to deploy manpower. It reflected how philosophically divided the two men were, how different they were in character.

Rizzo came to view Leary as a shivering coward, a man unfit to head an urban police department whose members faced violence and death as a matter of routine.

"He was a phony faker," Rizzo was to say later. "He wouldn't even come out of his office. If something happened after he went home, he didn't want to hear about it. He didn't want to be disturbed."*

Mayor Tate held similar convictions about Leary.

"He was funny. He was a loner, hard to reach. I know that he resisted even putting a police radio in his car because he wanted to be alone. I would try to call him, and when I couldn't get through he would later explain that he didn't know I was trying to reach him. I finally insisted on his getting a radio, but even then he resisted. Other times he would lock himself in his office and see no one. But he could surprise you. I went to the opera at the Academy of Music one night and Leary was there. I told him I didn't know he liked the opera and he replied, 'I don't. I just wanted a night off.' After he went to New York, Mayor Lindsay asked me if I ever had trouble contacting Leary. 'I knew it would get that way,' I told Lindsay."

Leary, on the other hand, considers Rizzo to be more flamboyant than effective; stripped of his rhetoric and political ties, he would be just another aggressive cop.

Leary defined the role of police commissioner as one con-

* Interview, September 1971.

sisting primarily of administrative duties. He was interested in the development of long-range concepts and programs and it was with this in mind that he first decided to reorganize the brass at the upper echelons. Leary's revision of the department's entire communications system made it one of the best in the nation. Each of the seven divisions has its own radio band. Two additional bands, known as "H" and "J," can broadcast throughout the department. With the help of computers, police response time has been cut to a maximum of two minutes, in most cases. Leary also instituted the controversial but unquestionably effective special units such as Intelligence, Civil Disobedience, and Labor Squads. Rizzo developed upon and enlarged many of these units and markedly increased the department's hardware—guns, walkie-talkies, lights, and sirens.

Rizzo generally is credited with instituting many of Leary's innovations. This disturbed the acquiescent commissioner, but he consistently declined to express his feelings. Indeed, Leary's frosty attitude toward the press and his reluctance to make personal appearances lost him many supporters within the community and the department.

Throughout the period of the Columbia Avenue riot, Rizzo remained on duty. He had been a virtual dynamo, jumping from trouble point to trouble point, encouraging his men, directing them himself, and frequently participating in arrests and shakedowns. He broke away to eat or rest briefly, but he was never far from the action. And this fact, in the long run, proved as significant as the open split between himself and Leary.

"You don't troubleshoot from a swivel chair" became his motto. With help from the media, Rizzo would draw upon this experience countless times in attempting to establish himself as the omnipresent cop.

"Did Frank Rizzo ever duck out?" he asked. "Did Frank

Rizzo take weekends off? Did he go to the shore and take it easy? Bet your ass he didn't. Frank Rizzo was on call twenty-four hours a day, seven days a week, three hundred sixty-five days a year. The people in this city know that. That's why they respect me."

And it was a fact. Frank Rizzo was a devoted cop. There were those who disagreed with his methods, those who thought him cruel and bigoted and disrespectful of points of view differing from his own. But no one ever accused Frank Rizzo of being dishonest with himself and not working at his job.

His presence in the front line did not go unnoticed by his men. Their feeling toward the boss was best summarized by an officer who worked under Rizzo for more than a decade.

"They'd walk barefoot over broken glass for him," the officer said. "They loved the guy."

Rizzo held equal affection for his men.

"I never asked them to do anything I wouldn't do myself," Rizzo explained. "They knew I was with them wherever the trouble was."

Moreover, Rizzo would defend his men against criticism and legal action even under the most questionable of circumstances. He would go to court and testify in their behalf. He would chastise anyone who criticized the police. If a policeman or a member of his family died, Rizzo would be at the wake. If a man was seriously injured in the line of duty, or off, Rizzo would be at the hospital. He would send flowers and offer personal condolences to relatives.

There were times when Leary attempted to put the brakes on Rizzo. One fall day in 1965 Rizzo moved in on a black teen-age boy who was picketing Girard College (a private high school for boys) on Girard Avenue in North Philadelphia. Rizzo was headed for the boy with a nightstick when Leary suddenly jumped in front of his deputy commissioner.

Leary got the blow instead. Rizzo later explained that it was an accident, that he couldn't stop his momentum.

On another fall day in 1965, Georgie Woods, a popular black disc jockey on radio station WDAS, who is active in community affairs, was driving along South Street when he came upon a brawl between whites and blacks. Woods quickly parked his car, telephoned the cops, and then attempted to use his prestige as a radio announcer to break up the fight. The police arrived in force—including Frank Rizzo, who had heard the call go out on the radio and had directed his driver, Sergeant John Devine, to take him to the scene.

Rizzo grabbed Woods and put a gun to his head.

"Make one move, you black son-of-a-bitch, and it'll take thirty-six doctors to put you back together."

Woods was arrested and charged with various things, including inciting a riot. Leary got word of the incident and called in Rizzo, who explained that he hadn't recognized Woods and that he thought the disc jockey was coming at him as if to attack. When informed of this, Woods agreed not to press charges if the books were wiped clean. Ironically, Woods held no grudge against Rizzo for the embarrassing incident.*

Reflecting on Rizzo more than five years later, Woods said, "I think he has been a good police commissioner. On the whole, he's done a good all-around job. There's resentment against him in the black community because of the treatment police have given the black man over the years, not only here but nationwide. I don't know if he's responsible for the polarization, but it does exist. I think that if I were police commissioner right now I would be resented, too. Whoever has the job would be resented. There are areas where Rizzo has made mistakes, particularly his public relations in the black community. The black community wants

* *Philadelphia Magazine*, July 1967, p. 79.

law and order, too, but we want it with justice. This is his biggest failing."*

Following the 1964 Columbia Avenue riot, the department began drawing up a massive set of contingency plans in the event of future civil disturbances.

One of Howard Leary's reasons for refusing to let Rizzo charge down Columbia Avenue that Friday night was that the police were outnumbered. That fact didn't particularly bother Frank Rizzo, but it disturbed Leary. The problem was one of logistics—how to get men to a given location in the shortest possible time and keep them mobile enough to be able to move to another point on a moment's notice.

Frank Rizzo later borrowed a tactic the French used in World War I, when Paris had been saved from the advancing German armies by French soldiers who were taken by taxis to the staging area for the Battle of the Marne. Rizzo's strategy for "saving" Philadelphia was to rent buses capable of carrying fifty armed policemen at a time. The buses were equipped with police radios so they could be summoned instantly, thus providing a strong back-up force for the various district commands. The department later purchased three of its own buses, which Rizzo used extensively.

"You have to have superior force," Rizzo explained. "Even if you don't have it, you can fake it. Like you can station a busload of cops in a conspicuous place. Or you can move the same busload around to various places. This way you create the impression that the cops are everywhere. It's possible to make fifty policemen look like a thousand if you handle it right."

To protect the policemen from snipers on rooftops, Leary and Rizzo developed a special team of sharpshooters who carried high-powered rifles equipped with telescopic sights. This team was originally known as the stake-out squad, and was primarily an antirobbery unit. Most of the team had been

* Interview, January 1971.

trained with .38-caliber service revolvers and sawed-off shotguns. But Rizzo pressed them into riot service and had them trained to fire the big rifles. Their job was to be on the lookout for snipers from rooftops, alleys, and windows.

Rizzo also began equipping many of his beat patrolmen with $800 walkie-talkies, giving them a direct radio link to the district headquarters. If a patrolman got into a serious jam, he could send out an "assist officer" call, giving his location. This would immediately be channeled through the district headquarters to the communications center at the Roundhouse, where an operator would then put out an "assist officer" call on the J-band. Within seconds of the original call, every on-duty policeman in Philadelphia would know that a fellow officer was in trouble and precisely where he was located. Officers in the immediate district would begin speeding to the scene. Reinforcements could be called for as needed, so that within minutes the buses could be on their way.

Rizzo would usually respond to serious calls and personally direct operations from the scene.

To assist in reconnaissance, the department worked out a leasing arrangement with Philadelphia International Airport for the use of helicopters. Rizzo fought to have the city buy the department its own helicopters, but he never succeeded. Nor could he persuade the City Council to appropriate money for the purchase of two bullet-proof personnel carriers, at an estimated cost of $30,000 each. These vehicles have wide rubber wheels instead of traditional tracks, and can cover themselves with foam if they are hit by a Molotov cocktail.

When Rizzo first made the request for the armored personnel carriers, the black community and liberal civic leaders immediately protested that Rizzo wanted "tanks." The name, however inaccurate, stuck, and the ensuing furor forced Mayor Tate to shelve the request.

The stake-out squad had been initiated in 1964, and Rizzo

continually expanded it and refined its operation. He increased its size from 30 to 115 men and stepped up their arms' training and target practice. He also beefed up the research and planning division of the department. Captain James Powers, an intelligent and sensitive man (he attends the opera and Philadelphia Orchestra concerts regularly), heads a unit of 4 sergeants, 5 civilians, and 16 policemen. Under Rizzo's orders, Powers and his staff completely reviewed the boundaries of all 326 patrol-car sectors on the basis of frequency of crime, and changed many of them.

Rizzo also instituted the policy of integrated patrol cars in areas with a large black population. No two patrolmen of the same race could operate together in these areas. And he increased the size of the K–9 patrol, with Captain Jack Auerback in charge. Under Auerback were 4 lieutenants, 4 sergeants, 68 K–9 patrolmen, and 68 dogs. He assigned the handlers and their dogs to the subways and elevated trains, but he would not permit them to be used for crowd-control or demonstrations.

The police never had to put their plans for counterinsurgency warfare into effect, at least not on a grand scale. There were minor disruptions and clashes, but nothing that could be accurately described as a major riot took place again. If it had, Rizzo would have been ready. As warm weather approached each spring, the police department was alert and tense.

In February 1966, Howard Leary—disenchanted with Philadelphia and still smarting from the criticism of his handling of the 1964 riot—resigned as police commissioner and took command of the New York City Police Department. Tate was less than sorry to see Leary step out and that feeling was shared by many men on the force, but his departure left Tate with the problem of picking a successor.

The odds on favorite seemed to be Frank Rizzo but the time wasn't right. The political winds were shifting and Tate, to keep peace with the ward heelers and the major-domos who finance the party, was forced to name a nominating panel to scour the country for the most qualified man.

"I knew I didn't have a chance," Rizzo said. "I got calls from a couple of people asking me to come before the panel for an interview, but I knew better. I had already gotten the word and there was no sense wasting my time."

Tate surprised almost everyone except Frank Rizzo by rejecting the candidates thrust on him by the special nominating panel. He turned instead to his old friend, Edward J. Bell, who was a deputy commissioner. Bell's tenure, however, was short-lived. Officially, he stayed on fifteen months, but he was ill during much of this time and Tate named Rizzo the acting commissioner.* Even when he was on the job, Bell sought Rizzo's advice on practically every major decision, according to Rizzo.

"He was weak," Rizzo said in an interview. "The man would get so afraid he couldn't even talk. He'd hide in his office and refuse to take phone calls."

That August, with racial tensions again running high and rumors spreading about armed black militants poised for trouble, Rizzo mobilized 80 heavily armed policemen, plus a reserve contingent of 1000, and raided four meeting places of the Student Non-Violent Coordinating Committee (SNCC). One of the raiding parties succeeded in turning up two and a half sticks of dynamite. The others did little more than stir up controversy.

James Foreman, national director of SNCC, charged that the "dynamite raids" were a frame-up. He claimed the police had planted the dynamite.†

* *Sunday Bulletin*, June 25, 1967.

† It was a likely possibility. In 1971 it was disclosed that police had been planting bags of heroin on suspected drug violators in order to bring them in for questioning. National SNCC chairman Stokely Carmichael came to a church in North Philadelphia and angrily told the congregation: "The next time Rizzo tries to march 1500 cops into our community, he's not going to get away with it."

Other militant black leaders voiced objections to the raids but the majority of the city's citizens thought Rizzo had performed a valuable service. It seemed inconsequential that charges against most of those arrested in the raids were dropped. All that seemed to matter was that Frank Rizzo was out there doing his job, "taking on" the "anarchists" who were bent on violence.

With the spring of 1967 came the Democratic mayoralty primary. Tate, whose popularity had declined since he had inherited the mayor's chair from Richardson Dilworth, found himself in trouble with the old-line Democratic power brokers. At the urging of Frank Smith, the Democratic City Committee Chairman, most of the ward leaders decided to forsake Tate for Alexander Hemphill, a capable politician who they felt might put the party back in the good graces of the people. But the politicians underestimated Tate. Just when they figured they had Tate all but beaten, the police began closing down bars faster than the ward leaders could say Carrie Nation. More than 200 were shut down in a few days. And it was no accident that the bars were located in the wards of those leaders who opposed Tate.

As an insurance measure, Tate announced on May 16 (the day of the primary) that Rizzo would be named as commissioner to replace Bell, whose retirement had been rumored for weeks.

Tate won the primary in a landslide. Bell resigned.

Five days later, more than 1000 persons jammed into Judge Joseph Sloane's courtroom to see Francis Lazzaro Rizzo, forty-six, take the oath of office as Police Commissioner of the City of Philadelphia. In the audience that day was the proudest father in town, Policeman Ralph Rizzo, retired.

"How do you think Dad looked?" Rizzo asked a friend shortly after he had been sworn in. "I think he could still pound a beat."

Less than a week later, Rizzo burned the last bridge between Leary and himself. Rizzo had never complained to Leary, had never been insubordinate, but now that he was running the show he wanted everyone to know where he stood.

In a small garden located outside the first-floor cafeteria of the Roundhouse, Leary had placed a five-ton granite rock as an aesthetic ornament to a small fountain. He had first seen the rock at a construction site on the Schuylkill Expressway and had arranged to have it brought to the Roundhouse. Understandably, it came to be known as "Leary's Rock."

Rizzo called in a crane and had it hauled away. Smiling broadly as it was being loaded onto a truck, he told reporters, "We're going to have the area sodded with grass."

Tate's announcement that he would appoint Rizzo commissioner unquestionably had some effects on the outcome of that election because there was little doubt that Rizzo had become a populist hero. To the vast majority of white residents, Rizzo represented the last line of defense between themselves and the blacks, who, they expected, might burn down the city at any time.

There were those, however—and they were a minority—who cringed at the thought of Frank Rizzo running the Philadelphia Police Department. The Civil Liberties Union's Spencer Coxe was one of them.

"I was simply appalled when he was made commissioner," Coxe said. "It seemed to me that he had exhibited none of the qualities of statesmanship and tact that the police commissioner should have. He didn't seem to understand disorder. His attitude was crush the opposition and this will take care of law and order."*

The events of that 1967 summer did not offer the mild-mannered Coxe much reassurance. He and twenty-one other persons were arrested outside the Cathedral of St. Peter and St. Paul in center city for violating a restriction on crowd size

* Interview in the *Evening Bulletin*, December 12, 1969.

that had been imposed after the Columbia Avenue riot. Rizzo, relying on reports on militants compiled by his Intelligence unit, charged that eight of twenty-two (not including Coxe) were "card-carrying Communists."*

November 17, 1967, was one of the most significant days in Frank Rizzo's career. It was a day of many things; of violence and misunderstanding; a day when those who held suspicions about Rizzo's penchant for violence had them confirmed; a day when those who considered him a "savior," a man of quick and decisive action, came away convinced they had witnessed the Second Coming.

That Friday, about 3500 Negro youths gathered at the School Administration offices at 21st Street and Benjamin Franklin Parkway in center city to hold a black-power demonstration. They had come to demand, among other things, more courses in Negro history and culture. Instead, they got a lesson on the street tactics of a hard-nosed cop named Frank L. Rizzo.

As the demonstration got under way, Rizzo sped to the scene. He stationed about 200 policemen around the crowd, while the demonstration leaders went inside the building to present their demands to Dr. Mark R. Shedd, the school superintendent, and several members of the Board of Education.

"They were very well behaved," Shedd said. "They wanted things that weren't totally unrealistic. We heard their demands and then went into a conference session to give them an answer."

Rizzo barged into the meeting, furious.

"He told me he was going to run my ass out of town," Shedd said.

Out in front of the building, the students waited. According to numerous observers, including reporters and various civic leaders, the group was peaceful. Two black members of

* *Sunday Bulletin*, January 12, 1969.

the school board, George Hutt and the Reverend Henry Nichols, moved among the demonstrators and the police, urging both sides to remain cool.

A few minutes later, a group of students climbed atop an automobile and ripped off a radio aerial. Rizzo, seeing the isolated incident, ordered his men to "get their asses," according to a *Philadelphia Inquirer* reporter, who was standing with Rizzo and other police officers. The police, apparently interpreting Rizzo's order as a general directive, swooped down on the entire crowd. Many students were chased for blocks as they attempted to run away. Others were beaten on the spot. When it was all over, approximately fifteen students and five policemen had been injured.

To this day, Rizzo insists that his men acted properly and he defends his handling of the situation.

"Look," he said, "I thought we handled ourselves well. We broke it up before it got out of hand. It might have been much worse if we had just stood by. I believe it is easier to blow out a match than extinguish a forest fire."*

But more than a few civic leaders and public officials were aghast. Richardson Dilworth, then president of the Board of Education, saw it this way: "There were no threats of disorder when all of a sudden 200 uniformed cops charged and went right through the crowd, whacking kids on the head . . . even while they were running away. A lot of innocent people got beaten because the police lost their heads."†

Coxe, who had observed the demonstration, called for federal intervention. He explained his action by saying, "Regardless of the rights or wrongs involved, when that demonstration began the police were under the command of Lieutenant Fencl [Lieutenant George Fencl, head of the Civil Disobedience Squad]. There was a lot of noise, the crowd was very large. But when Rizzo took charge, there was a dramatic

* Interview, September 1971.
† *Philadelphia Inquirer*, November 18, 1967.

change in police behavior. He gave orders to clear out the demonstration. The police had been acting very properly and with restraint. But after he arrived, they acted, I think, with great brutality. I saw some of this myself. The police were not provoked by the students. Of course, there were incidents that warranted police activity. I saw two students jump on a car and break the aerial. The police took their cue from the commissioner and their character changed in response to his wishes. That's the frightening thing about the police establishment. Its members don't seem to have any moral sense of their own. They do what they're told to do, what they're ordered to do."

The combined leadership of the local NAACP called for Rizzo's immediate removal and commended Dilworth and Shedd for "having the courage to tell the truth regarding the Gestapo-like actions of the police."

More than 800 Negroes held a meeting in a West Philadelphia church the following Sunday night and voted to boycott public schools and white merchants until Rizzo was fired. The Community Legal Services filed suit in federal court seeking Rizzo's ouster. After lengthy testimony, the suit was dismissed and the United States Supreme Court subsequently refused to hear an appeal. Other civil-rights activists, such as attorney Cecil B. Moore, a long-time Rizzo critic and one of the most flamboyant and influential black leaders in the city, also called for Rizzo's firing.

But there were many who came to the commissioner's defense. John Harrington, national president of the 200,000-member Fraternal Order of Police, said if that Rizzo was fired, "we policemen would just turn our heads, collect our pay, and let the people police themselves." Then, turning the tables, Harrington and the executive committee of the FOP sent a letter to Mayor Tate calling for the ouster of Shedd, Dilworth, and the Reverend Nichols.

"We need new members on the Board of Education,"

Harrington said, "because if Dick Dilworth wants to be the Pied Piper of anarchy and permit students—thousands of them—to take off from school and demonstrate in the streets, then it's plain the board is surrendering. We feel there's too much damn surrendering taking place and there's too much anarchy in the streets today."

In the midst of the furor Mayor Tate cut short a vacation in Florida to return to Philadelphia and defend his police commissioner. It had been his support of Rizzo that had won the election for him only ten days before. It seemed the very least he could do in return.

"Rizzo," the mayor announced, "is the best law-enforcement officer in the land."

Even the Board of Education, whose members are appointed by the mayor and serve without pay, was openly split over the issue. While Dilworth and the Reverend Nichols strongly criticized Rizzo, three members who were closely aligned with the Democratic machine defended the commissioner's actions, saying that his quick response had probably prevented further violence.

By the time the storm subsided, Rizzo was still in charge of the Philadelphia Police Department and he had unquestionably become the most controversial and well-known public figure in Philadelphia. This was precisely what he wanted.

To his admirers, Rizzo had become "Supercop," the toughest law-and-order man ever to wear a badge, the man who saved them from the forces of evil. To his detractors, Rizzo was a racist megalomaniac who wanted nothing more than to place the city under a permanent state of martial law.

The real Frank Rizzo fell somewhere between these two extremes, but he was quite content to be judged in this manner because he had many more admirers than detractors.

The city, then, had become polarized concerning Rizzo and the police, and much of it by his own design. By eliminating the dispassionate middle ground of opinion, Rizzo felt that people would have to choose between law and order on the one hand, and lawlessness and chaos on the other. If you were for Frank Rizzo, you stood up for law and order; if you criticized him, you were a "coddler of criminals."

Just when the dust was beginning to settle, when the issue had spun itself out, Rizzo and the politicians at City Hall staged one of their shabbier spectacles. They went after a liquorless psychedelic night club known as the Electric Factory, and it was the coffeehouse raids of a decade earlier all over again.

The Electric Factory, owned by two brothers, Joseph and Allen Spivak, opened in February 1968 in a converted tire factory at 22nd and Arch Streets, in center city. There are insiders who say that Rizzo was acting on the wishes of Mayor Tate, who was personally affronted by the Factory operating within the shadow of City Hall. There are others—mainly policemen—who say the Factory became a focal point for the sale and use of drugs, and this prompted Rizzo to move against it.

Whatever the reason, Philadelphia police, under Rizzo's command, began a harassment campaign against the club that lasted for months. He detached Sergeant Francis Bayer of the Intelligence Security Unit to conduct a confidential investigation in April, May, and June 1968. Bayer employed units of the highway patrol, district command, the wagon crew, and sector cars. There also were three undercover agents from the Juvenile Aid Division in on the investigation as well as a member of the narcotics unit, who spent twenty-five evenings at the Factory.

Despite the presence of all these gumshoes, the investigation produced little. There were several arrests, including that of a band member who was booked for possession of marijuana after the police caught him smoking it in a pipe while sitting in a car. On two other occasions, there were arrests for violation of the casually enforced curfew law, which prohibits youths under eighteen from being on the streets after 10:30 p.m. during the week, and midnight on Friday and Saturday.

On the basis of this paltry evidence, Rizzo requested the late Judge Joseph Sloane, then seventy-one and the man who had sworn him into office, to close down the Factory.

The judge obliged, using the following immortal logic: "This place of amusement is not a place of quiet mirth and enjoyment. Unlike the Academy of Music, where one hears the orchestras of Toscanini and Stokowski or Ormandy, the Electric Factory caters to other groups known variously as the Peanut Butter Conspiracy, the Vanilla Fudge, and the Jefferson Airplane, or Country Joe and the Fish to name but a few, and lends itself to the rise and fall of loud sounds."

To the surprise of practically no one, the ruling was overturned on appeal. The Factory remained open until early 1970, when it died of natural causes; to wit, it went broke.

Rizzo's treatment of the Factory and the men who owned it (he had warned Allen Spivak that he would convert the establishment "into a parking lot") sadly disillusioned those who thought he had become more tolerant over the years.

But while surveillance of the Factory was taking place, Rizzo convinced even his sternest critics that he was capable of restraint.

Dr. Martin Luther King, Jr., was assassinated in Memphis, Tennessee, in April that year and black ghettos in cities throughout the country suddenly boiled over with violence and hatred. Philadelphia, it appeared, was on the verge of exploding.

Many feared the worst as thousands of infuriated and grieving blacks poured into Independence Mall to pay homage to the slain civil-rights leader. But it didn't happen, partly

Rafael "Ralph" Rizzo and his four sons, from left: Anthony, Joseph, Ralph, and Frank (circa 1930). *Photo by Philadelphia Inquirer*

A common scene at the old 12th and Pine Streets station house: Rizzo arguing with a lawyer before the magistrate. Rizzo in his early days as a policeman was often accused of ignoring the finer points of the law when making arrests. *Photo by Philadelphia Inquirer*

Captain Frank Rizzo consults with his lawyer, the late State Senator Benjamin J. Donolow, who represented him several times in "brutality" cases. The uniformed men were Navy corpsmen who claimed that Rizzo and another officer had beaten them. Rizzo, as usual, was cleared of the charges. The incident occurred in August 1955. *Photo by Philadelphia Inquirer*

Captain Rizzo and an unidentified police officer with an illegal still captured during a raid (circa 1955). Rizzo, who made it a point to cultivate newspapermen, always got good coverage in the Philadelphia papers. *Photo by Philadelphia Inquirer*

Rizzo prided himself on being at the scene of the action when there was trouble. Here, he wades into the thick of a civil disturbance between white and black residents in the Tasker Homes area of South Philadelphia. *Photo by Philadelphia Inquirer*

Rizzo briefs two helmeted policemen assigned to a civil rights demonstration at John F. Kennedy Plaza in Center City. *Photo by Philadelphia Inquirer*

After he became Police Commissioner, Rizzo used Car One on an almost nightly cruise of Philadelphia's expected trouble spots. His driver is Sergeant John Devine. *Photo by Philadelphia Inquirer*

This picture, published on the front page of the *Philadelphia Daily News* in August 1970, touched off a furor. The police had raided the headquarters of the Black Panthers in West Philadelphia. Black-power groups charged that the police forced the suspects to strip; others claimed that the Panthers stripped voluntarily, hoping to embarrass Rizzo. Rizzo was not present when the raid was conducted. *Photo by Philadelphia Daily News*

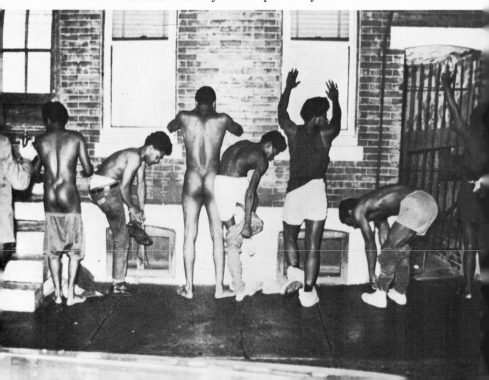

With a nightstick stuck in his cummerbund, Police Commissioner Rizzo helped quell a civil disturbance in South Philadelphia on June 12, 1969. He had been a dinner guest at a political rally when the alarm went out. *Photo by Philadelphia Daily News*

At a news conference in the Police Administration Building, Police Commissioner Rizzo displays a weapon allegedly used in a homicide in 1970. The placing of the shield behind him was a Rizzo touch: it showed prominently in all photographs. *Photo by Philadelphia Inquirer*

Election night, November 2, 1971. Rizzo, standing beside former mayor James H. J. Tate, tells a wildly cheering crowd that "only in America could a guy like Frank Rizzo be elected mayor...." *Photo by Philadelphia Inquirer*

Rizzo on the morning of November 3, 1971. *Photo by Philadelphia Inquirer*

A K-9 patrol in front of Mayor Rizzo's house on Provident Road in the Mount Airy section of Philadelphia. About ten months after his election Rizzo started building a new home in the Roxborough section on a wooded six-acre tract. The cost was a reputed $114,000. *Photo by Philadelphia Inquirer*

Two views of Rizzo during a news conference, shortly after he was elected Mayor of Philadelphia. *Photos by Philadelphia Daily News*

Rizzo in his home with his pet Yorkshire terrier, Oliver. *Photo by Philadelphia Inquirer*

The Rizzo family: Francis, Jr.; Rizzo's wife, Carmella; Rizzo; and his daughter, Joanna. The picture was taken soon after Rizzo's election as mayor. *Photo by Philadelphia Daily News.*

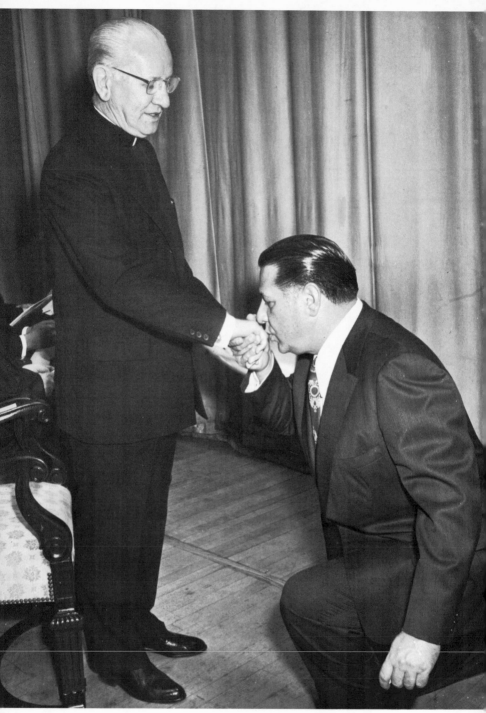

Mayor Frank Rizzo and John Cardinal Krol, Archbishop of Philadelphia.
Photo by Philadelphia Daily News

because black leaders spent long hours calming the marchers, and partly because Frank Rizzo kept his cool.

"The police acted with great propriety," said Coxe. "They acted with great restraint, as did Rizzo. There were no incidents. In that particular instance, Rizzo couldn't have been improved upon."

Had the situation gotten out of hand, however, Rizzo would have been ready and the results could have been disastrously different. Rizzo had his men hiding in buses on side streets out of sight of the mall area.

Not long afterward Rizzo showed again that he was capable of riding herd on his emotions, even under the most trying conditions. In August 1970 the People's Constitutional Convention opened at Temple University's McGonigle Hall in the heart of the North Philadelphia black ghetto.

The personal strain on the commissioner was enormous. The convention, which drew 5000 persons, many of them radicals from across the country, came smack on the heels of a bloody and savage weekend in which a Fairmount Park police sergeant was murdered in a park guardhouse, two other officers were gunned down in a patrol wagon, two more were critically shot when they stopped a car for questioning, and three more were injured during a raid on Black Panther headquarters.

Rizzo was justifiably outraged. The shootings and killings were cold-blooded. Policemen had been shot down without warning or provocation.

"Yellow dogs," he screamed at them over television, daring them into the streets for a shoot-out. "We'll give them ten to our three."

With Rizzo in this frame of mind, it was little wonder that most people feared the People's Constitutional Convention would touch off a bloodbath.

To Rizzo's credit, it did not. Although more than 1000

heavily armed policemen were stationed throughout the city, particularly in the neighborhood of Temple University, they were practically invisible to the conventioneers. The convention leaders, in turn, stayed out of Rizzo's way. And the weekend came and went without incident.

"I know how to keep my cool," Rizzo explained two years later. "I've been in tough situations all my life. These liberal bastards think they're going to get me hot every time they open their mouth. But it's not going to happen. I save it for when I need it. And they know that, too. They know they can't push Frank Rizzo too far. Like the pukes who shot those policemen [in 1970]. No excuse for that. I would have met them anywhere they wanted to meet. Guns, fists, made no difference to me. I'd give them a three-to-one advantage and take 'em all. And I'd still do it. Any time they're ready."

Rizzo appeared to have come a long way from that black power rally at the School Administration Building in 1967. The fact that the People's Constitutional Convention came off without incident made many of the city's liberal leaders and black spokesmen concede that Rizzo had made a determined effort to establish a better relationship with the black community.

He had even taken punitive action against policemen who were guilty of indiscretions. During the convention, for example, he had been informed that while riding in a car, three white detectives had shouted racial slurs at conference participants. Rizzo immediately suspended the three men pending an investigation, and when one of them admitted the charge, Rizzo suspended him for fifteen days without pay.

"The feeling I get," said Murray Freidman, executive director of the American Jewish Committee, "is that there's been real improvement in the police since November 17, 1967. We liberals have generally consigned the police to the tender ministrations of the Birch Society. The need exists for liberals and well-intentioned whites generally to recognize the legitimate aspirations of the police. We all have much to gain from a more effective police force."*

William S. Rawls, the former head of the Urban League of Philadelphia, said in January 1968 that Rizzo "was the face of the police state," adding that he was more alarmed by the Philadelphia Police Commissioner than he was by H. Rap Brown, the black radical.

A year later, Rawls saw things quite differently.

"It would appear to me that Rizzo recently has made considerable effort to develop better relations with the black community. I haven't seen anything that he's done in recent months that could be considered inflammatory."

There were those, however, whose evaluations of Rizzo remained unchanged. Philip Savage, former director of the NAACP for Pennsylvania, New Jersey, and Delaware, was not at all impressed by Rizzo's apparently conciliatory attitude toward blacks and militant liberals.

"The tone of his tenure as commissioner has been highly antidemocratic, antijudicial, and more in line with the way in which punishment was meted out during pioneer days," Savage said. "Rizzo's utterances have made it almost impossible for anyone accused to get a fair trial. He calls accused persons 'creeps' and 'animals'! These labels tend to prejudge the innocence or guilt of persons, thereby serving to undermine our whole judicial process. Those like Rizzo who tend to inculcate antidemocratic feelings among uninitiated segments of our community weaken the democratic process. Rizzo represents to whites the protection against black political take-over—the only barrier protecting them against barbaric, animalistic actions of blacks, the kind of crap whites have been taught to believe about blacks. To that extent Rizzo has been a promoter and exponent of black hatred. I don't believe he is antiblack, personally. I don't believe that it's intended. He's unaware of his actions and expressions and he can't

* *Evening Bulletin*, January 12, 1969.

control them. This tends to promote hatred of students, blacks, radicals, and those accused of crimes."*

To the vast majority of Philadelphians, however, Rizzo was nothing short of a Messiah. The row-house dwellers, the thousands upon thousands of working-class people who constitute the bulk of the city's population, felt Rizzo had saved them from the horrible rioting that had racked almost every other major city in America. Frank Rizzo was Philadelphia's Horatio Alger, the embodiment of the Protestant ethic, the personification of the law-and-order issue. For every Spencer Coxe and Philip Savage there were 100 just plain people. Rizzo knew it, and he gauged his actions accordingly. If you disagreed with Frank Rizzo and the way he ran the police department, then you were against law and order. You were a knee-jerk liberal.

Jack Levine, a lawyer for Philadelphians for Equal Justice, said, "Rizzo is exceptionally moral on the life-style issue. The people on the top can affect the men under them. Rizzo doesn't like long hair, beards, and bell-bottom pants, so the men don't either. He's personalized those issues. But police attitudes in other cities aren't really any different. The significant thing about Rizzo is that he has become the personification of law and order. He has a tremendous amount of charisma. When you see Rizzo, you feel a tremendous personal presence. Brutality didn't come with Frank Rizzo. But for the cops on the beat, Rizzo exemplifies that attitude. My personal impression of Rizzo is that he is a really smooth operator. He has a magical way of disarming people. Rizzo is the product of the urban stresses at work, not the cause of them. He really believes his solutions are the solutions for the city."†

The praise most often heard for Rizzo is that he prevented a recurrence of the Columbia Avenue riot—that he kept

* Interview, January 1971
† Interview, January 1971.

Philadelphia cool when other cities burned. Most black leaders seriously question that contention.

Mary Rouse, a rotund black woman who is president of the Kensington Black Affairs Council, has been instrumental in initiating several brutality suits against Rizzo and the police department. Rizzo, she has often said, is the source of much of the racial tension, not the instrument for easing it.

"There has been a marked increase in police brutality under Rizzo," she said "I know that under Gibbons, Leary, and Bell it was different. We didn't have as many problems under the other commissioners. Rizzo is a very shrewd man. A lot of blacks think he's just another dropout. But he has made this a city of fear. He has whites afraid of blacks and blacks suspicious of each other. I make no distinction between black and white policemen because young people tell me black policemen are tougher on the brothers in order not to offend their white partners. I can't think of anything that happens where he isn't on the scene. He's got to mete out the punishment. Kensington is just like Hattiesburg, Mississippi."*

Savage maintains that the presence of police in large numbers often serves as a catalyst to violence:

"Repressed people don't care about guns, police, blood shedding. If anything, the overreaction by police tends to promote the causes of repressed people. It's not fair to say Rizzo kept the lid on. It's been the black leaders who have done the work. Take the King incident. This city avoided racial turmoil because we held a meeting that night calling on the public to be peaceful. We also sponsored two highly supported demonstrations deploring the assassination. This action gave the black community a nonviolent avenue for venting their resentment. It wasn't the fact that policemen were in garrison, ready to pounce on the demonstrators. The same is true of the black-power convention. The NAACP called for public demonstrations denouncing Rizzo's raid

* Interview, January 1971.

on the Black Panthers' office. There would have been trouble if we hadn't, regardless of whether Rizzo armed cops to the teeth. His saying he controlled the riot situation is a typical self-serving statement. This city could have blown up two or three times if it hadn't been for the fact that reasonable blacks avoided supporting marginal issues and steps taken by more militant blacks."

The infamous police raids on the three Black Panther headquarters in August 1970 have been a source of controversy, misunderstanding, and misinformation. Much of it stemmed from a picture (taken by Elwood P. Smith, a photographer for the *Philadelphia Daily News*) that appeared on the front page of the tabloid newspaper several hours after the raids took place.

The picture showed six nude Panthers leaning with outstretched arms against a wall, their bare buttocks facing the camera. A fully clothed female was among the group. The paper no sooner hit the streets than his opponents charged that Rizzo had conducted the raids and that he forced the Panthers to strip nude on the street to humiliate them. That story still held sway as late as 1971, when *The New York Times*, in a report on the Democratic mayoralty primary that year, again rehashed this totally erroneous version of what transpired.

Frank Rizzo did not participate in the raid. He had been at the Roundhouse until approximately 1:30 a.m. that morning, helping plan three simultaneous raids on the Panther headquarters. He then went home and went to bed.

Charles Montgomery, a former reporter for the *Evening Bulletin* and *Daily News* who went along on the raid in question, gave this version, substantiated by John J. McGuire, a *Daily News* reporter who was also present. At 6 a.m. under a light drizzle, thirty policemen comprising elements of the stake-out squad, the detective division, and the highway patrol, led by Inspector Robert Kopsitz of Internal Security, arrived at a Panther headquarters which was located in a two-story row house at 3625 Wallace Street, in West Philadelphia.

At this same time, other raiding parties were arriving at 29th Street and Columbia Avenue, in North Philadelphia, and at a high-rise apartment building at 300 West Queen Lane, in Germantown. Priority had been given the Wallace Street location as it was considered the central headquarters, and police believed the occupants to be heavily armed.

Kopsitz drew his service revolver, stood to the side of the door, banged on it, and yelled for the occupants to come out. There was no reply for several minutes; then suddenly a shotgun was fired from a second-story window. Police and reporters began taking cover and shots were exchanged between the Panthers and the police for approximately two minutes. Kopsitz repeatedly yelled for the Panthers to come out, that the police had a warrant. Getting no response he moved toward the door again, but as he was poised ready to force it open, a shot crackled through the wood. Kopsitz then hollered out for someone to radio an "assist officer" and to bring an ax.

Montgomery crawled to a nearby red car, and radioed for help. As he was making the transmission, another "assist officer" call was radioed from 29th and Columbia, where three policemen had been wounded. Within minutes, police responded to the Wallace Street call.

Kopsitz continued yelling through a bullhorn for the occupants to surrender. After approximately twenty-five minutes, a voice was heard saying, "All right, we're coming out."

Before anyone emerged, the inspector ordered weapons to be thrown out first. Out came a shotgun, followed by a man who was put against the wall. Next, a .30-caliber rifle was thrown from the top of the stairs; it broke at the stock when it hit the pavement. Although a shell was in the chamber, it was not discharged. The lone female then came out, followed by three more men. The last man to emerge held a rifle at his hip. Police ordered him to drop it, but as he stepped clear of the doorway, he seemed to be taking aim. Captain Alfonso Giordano fired a shot over the man's head, and the weapon fell to the sidewalk.

Some of the occupants of the house were barefoot, others were bare-chested. A female detective led the woman to a van where she was searched and then brought back to the wall. Police, meanwhile, began searching the men. In the midst of the shouting, an order was given for the men to loosen their pants to facilitate the search. Instead, they took them off and then removed their underwear, until they stood nude, hands again against the wall. Smith took his picture, police completed their search, and the men were told to dress. They were then taken away.

V

Meanwhile, There Is the Man to Consider

The word passed quickly through the grapevine of the Central Police District in June 1964 that Frank "Birdman" Phelan, a notorious local thug, had heard quite enough about Inspector Frank Rizzo. He wanted to take on Rizzo and see who was tougher.

Within hours, the police picked up Phelan and brought him in for questioning. Rizzo escorted Phelan to a room and closed the door behind them.

"I heard you've been looking for me," Rizzo snarled.

Phelan seemed surprised by the size and demeanor of his adversary. But he quickly regained his composure and the two men squared off. Phelan threw a punch to the jaw of the inspector. Rizzo ducked, and as he rose he brought with him a left uppercut that started somewhere near his shoes and ended with a dull thud against Phelan's neck.

Phelan fell back against a wall gasping for breath. As he slid to the floor, hand at his throat, he gurgled forth the information police had been trying to gather for days.

Phelan admitted he had been hired by a man named

Jack Lopinson to kill his wife, Judy, and his boss, Joseph "Flowers" Molito.

Both Phelan and Lopinson were convicted for the 1964 murders and Rizzo, relating the tale to friends eight years later, commented, "God works in strange ways."

SECURITY IS VERY TIGHT at the Police Administration Building. Only one entrance to the three-story edifice at 8th and Race Streets remains open, although there are numerous doors. That is the one in the rear facing a parking lot and just inside sits a cop at a desk. He is equipped with a gun, a logbook, a clock, and a hidden alarm for summoning police from all over the building. His job is to see that every visitor signs in and out and logs the time.

The building, commonly called the Roundhouse, is shaped like a dumbbell—two circular structures of concrete and glass joined by a narrow corridor. A high, prefabricated concrete wall surrounds the building except for the main entrance doors on the Race Street side, which are closed, and the rear entrance, which is guarded.

The police commissioner's office is on the third floor of the building. Like the rear entrance, the corridor leading to his office is guarded by a policeman who mans a logbook. At the other end of the corridor are a bevy of assistants and secretaries who comprise his staff.

The Roundhouse is coldly utilitarian in design. It has an antiseptic quality about it, a lifeless rigidity that is only slightly humanized by the movements of hundreds of intense-looking men, mostly in trench coats and pork-pie hats.

Frank L. Rizzo spent the most dramatic years of his life as the highest-ranking man in this building. He held forth from this fortress as the most controversial, perhaps most powerful man in Philadelphia.

Rizzo and the Roundhouse became synonymous. He was not commissioner when it was built in 1963, but it is thought of as his building. Although he has been out of it for many months, his presence is still very much felt in its myriad offices and corridors.

Frank Rizzo was more than the top cop at the Roundhouse. He was the patriarchal monarch of the 7200-man police force, a man who demanded the respect accorded a general, but who enjoyed playing the role of a lieutenant and personally leading his men into the fray.

At one moment he might be seated comfortably at his large desk, affixing his signature to an administrative order; the next moment he might be running toward Car One, to speed to the scene of an incident he felt demanded his personal attention.

Rizzo would assemble and deploy an entire stake-out squad and establish patterns for rerouting traffic. Then, perhaps wearing a helmet and face mask, he would lead the pursuit— whether it was a man with a gun, 50 violent demonstrators, or 100 rioting prisoners.

When it was all over, he would return to the Roundhouse, change shirts, get into a clean suit, dust off his shoes, and continue wading through his paperwork.

There was no engagement so important it could not be interrupted. Nothing at home was so pressing that he wouldn't leave to be at the scene of an incident.

On the night of June 12, 1969, for example, Rizzo was at the Bellevue-Stratford Hotel in center city attending a formal banquet in honor of Mayor James H. J. Tate.

At approximately 9:30 p.m., as the speeches droned on and the drinks continued to flow, a band of white youths crossed over into a black block in South Philadelphia near the explosive intersection of 25th and Tasker Streets and began throwing rocks and bottles at windows.

Two blocks away, a black gang invaded a white block and began dancing on cars, yelling obscenities, and threatening the residents.

By the time the first police cars arrived and Rizzo had been informed of the seriousness of the situation, the size of the two roving gangs was well over 100. Unless stopped, they were sure to clash. Bloodshed was inevitable.

Rizzo left the dinner at the Bellevue-Stratford, grabbed his driver, Sergeant John Devine, and took off. At 25th and Tasker Streets he climbed out of the car, stuck a nightstick in his cummerbund, and walked into the midst of a milling crowd of black youths.

"Do me a favor," he told them. "Go to your homes."

He got a negative response.

"Please," he said, "please go to your homes."

Slowly they began moving away.

Rizzo continued walking down the middle of Tasker Street. He turned up Bailey Street between 26th and 27th Streets where he was confronted by a crowd of about 300 white residents.

They cheered and applauded Rizzo, but when he asked them to disperse, they kept moving forward reaching out to touch him.

"Look at me," Rizzo said attempting to ease the tensions, "a poor Italian boy from South Philadelphia in a two-hundred-dollar tuxedo."

Finally, with the help of a Catholic priest from nearby St. Aloysius Church, he persuaded them to go home. Rizzo then gathered his top brass and, in the glow of a mercury-vapor street light, mapped plans to keep extra men on duty in the tense area.

"I know, I know," he quipped, "we'll have to ask for another $8 million. But tonight we've got to keep the men in here."

Three youths were arrested, but there was no clash. A potential tragedy had been averted. By midnight the neighborhood was again resting under an uneasy calm.

This was the Frank Rizzo most Philadelphians came to know and love. This was Frank Rizzo, "Supercop," the man who kept things cool. They knew Frank Rizzo was always there. They knew because they could see him nightly on television, or read about him almost every day in the newspapers.

But one need go no further than the man himself to get this assessment. Frank Rizzo will gladly tell you how tough a cop he was and what a great job he did as police commissioner. He will tell you how he grabbed his bootstraps back in South Philadelphia thirty years ago and how he has been pulling at them ever since. He will tell you how hard he works at being mayor of all the people, how he is going to turn the city around, how he is going to bring the races together. He will say all this with little provocation because one of Frank Rizzo's favorite people is Frank Rizzo.

I first met Rizzo on a cold rainy day in January 1971, about two months before he announced his candidacy. With a fellow reporter from the *Daily News* I had gone to Rizzo's office at the Roundhouse to conduct the first of several interviews for a series of articles about him.

There were three reporters in his office when we arrived, which was not unusual at 10 a.m. By that time in the morning Rizzo had usually gone through the mail, signed whatever papers there were, been briefed by Deputy Commissioners Robert Selfridge and Morton Solomon, and was ready for the press and his appointments.

Rizzo was pacing the floor, regaling his audience with one-liners about lenient judges, politics, and the upcoming Democratic mayoral primary.

"Come in, come in," he said, spotting us in the doorway.

Following a round of introductions, the other three reporters left. Rizzo then began pushing a large plastic pad beneath his desk with his foot. He would lean the great hulk of his body forward, keeping the heel of his shoe locked against the pad, and then slowly rock back and forth as if trying to adjust its position. He does this frequently to relieve cramps in his legs.

"You know I don't need this," he said of our intention to write the articles. "Are you gonna talk to Spencer Coxe and Father Gracie? If you are I don't want any part of it. Forget it right now."

Spencer Coxe, head of the Philadelphia Chapter of the American Civil Liberties Union, and the Reverend David Gracie, an Episcopal minister who came to Philadelphia from Detroit, have been thorns in Rizzo's side for years. Father Gracie has been active in the peace movement and has helped organize numerous marches and demonstrations.

"We have a little march planned for Sunday," Reverend Gracie will say. "We're going to put barbed wire around the crib of Jesus and station armed guards . . . symbolic of oppression."

We attempted to explain to Rizzo that we wanted him to tell us his positions instead of getting them secondhand from someone else. He had heard that argument before.

"Look," he shouted, "people know what I stand for. They know Frank Rizzo. Known him for years. What do you guys wanna do this for, anyway?"

Rizzo had already been told by half a dozen sources precisely what we were doing, and he knew that the newspaper would begin running the articles the day after he announced his candidacy for the primary. In fact, it was Harry R. Belinger, then city editor of the *Daily News* and one of Rizzo's closest friends, who had talked Rizzo into going along with the interviews.

Rizzo, of course, was right. He didn't need the publicity. He was making the papers almost daily through his work as commissioner, and most of that news was controlled. The stories emanating from the Roundhouse generally went something like this:

"Police Commissioner Frank L. Rizzo arrived at the scene minutes after . . ."

Or:

"Rizzo took command of the situation. . . ."

Neither of us expected Rizzo to be cooperative during the first interview. At best, we hoped to break the ice. Rizzo smacked through it like the SS *Manhattan*.

"Phony fuckin' liberals," he suddenly blurted out. "All I hear is a lot of goddamned talk."

With that he moved his feet off the plastic pad and pointed toward a conference room just off his office.

"Let's go in there," he said, striding to the door.

The conference room was as antiseptic as the operating room at St. Luke's Hospital, where he had undergone an operation for hemorrhoids a few weeks before. While such intimate medical details are usually bypassed by editors, in Rizzo's case the event had been front-page news with large headlines.

It is a big, plain room (Rizzo does not like pictures on walls) with paneled walls and a red carpet. We sat at a long, highly polished conference table, with Rizzo at its head. He was positioned in such a way that the large wall model of the shield of the department, with the words "Honor, Integrity, Service," was just behind and slightly above him.

This was another of the Rizzo touches. It was particularly effective when Rizzo was being photographed, filmed, or televised. The viewer could see only Rizzo and the shield.

As we talked, Rizzo went through a sequence of movements that are peculiarly his. He pulled at the sleeves of his blue pin-striped suit until the cuffs of his shirt and jeweled cuff links were protruding just the right distance. Buttoning and unbuttoning the coat, he moved his neck up and down inside his size 19½ shirt collar. Then he twisted his head left and right, jutting his jaw forward. His hamlike hands, with fingers as thick as frankfurters, opened and closed and thumped the table. Often he moved them to the sides of his head, slicking back his shiny black hair. And all the while he moistened his lips, pulling them between his teeth and pushing them out again, rolling one under the other.

We were in his office for more than an hour. We asked him five, maybe six questions—an indication of how Rizzo can dominate a conversation.

"What do you want me to tell you?"

I started to answer but he quickly said: "Crime. You want to hear about crime? I'll tell you about crime. If the courts don't start putting the criminals in prisons, this city, this country, is going to fall apart. We break our asses locking up these hoodlums and the liberal judges let them out. Not one, two, or three times. Fifteen times. We got guys on parole who have been arrested for the same thing a dozen times. Is that crime? Let me tell you something . . ."

With that he paused rose to his feet and went to the window. He buttoned and unbuttoned his coat, and then turned to look out at the rain pounding on the streets below. Suddenly he wheeled around.

"You know why I'm going to run for mayor? Because I'm the only guy who can save this city. I know it. The people know it. And the politicians know it. That's why they're falling all over each other trying to throw in with me.

"These liberal bastards—don't get me wrong, it's not the liberals I mind, it's the dewy-eyed liberals—they'd give their ass to be in my position."

Rizzo was shouting at this point. He was the evangelist of law and order, an Elmer Gantry at a political Armageddon. His arms were outstretched and his barrel chest was expanded. Neither of us would have been greatly surprised if the rains had suddenly stopped and the sun had come streaming through the windows.

Suddenly Rizzo fell quiet. He walked back to the table and sat down.

"You guys wanna know about Frank Rizzo?" he started again, as if he were talking about someone else. "I'll tell you about Frank Rizzo. Frank Rizzo came up the hard way, all right? Is that what you wanna hear? You wanna hear about how Frank Rizzo never robbed anybody in his life? How he never took anything that didn't belong to him? How he never mugged anybody or snatched an old lady's purse? Is that it?"

He was wearing a smile of confidence at this point because this is Rizzo at his best. It is a speech he has made to countless people, his vision of himself as Horatio Alger.

"Frank Rizzo hasn't taken a vacation in four years. Worked sixteen hours a day. Didn't hide in his office when there was trouble. Gave the taxpayers their money's worth.

"They accuse me of being against civil rights. That's not so. I'm a liberal when it comes to human rights. My heritage wouldn't let me be anything else. But I'm a conservative when it comes to crime. I'm against it. And I don't think a guy who's been convicted time after time for crimes of violence should be allowed to walk the streets."

Rizzo grabbed me at the forearm, leaned over, and said laughingly; "When I'm elected mayor I'm going to give the Henry Avenue Bridge concession to one of the reporters. He'll charge six-fifty a head to the liberals who want to jump off. He'll make a fortune."

Rizzo could have gone on for hours. But on this particular day he had to attend a luncheon to accept a "Man of the Year Award" from a South Philadelphia civic group.

We returned to his office and Rizzo took off his coat, removed his shoulder holster with the .38-caliber service revolver, and unfastened his cuff links.

"I gotta run, now," he said. "No Spencer Coxe or Father Gracie, right?"

"We'll be fair," I replied.

Meanwhile, There Is the Man to Consider || 101

"Fuck the fair stuff," he said. "I don't want no part of this if you're gonna talk to those liberal phonies. All right?"

We said nothing. Rizzo walked toward the bathroom that adjoins his office, to change shirts and comb his hair. It was still pouring rain that afternoon when we caught a taxi and headed for the office of the Reverend David Gracie.

The image of Rizzo that has been honed by the news media over the years is one of toughness. He was the "Cisco Kid," and then "Supercop"—a hard-charging, club-swinging policeman who had little regard for the rights of the accused.

There is abundant evidence to support that image. But it is a one-dimensional image. Rizzo is clearly a man with a multifaceted personality, and even his critics recognize this.

"There is no doubt Rizzo is a hard-driving character," says Spencer Coxe. "He's a complex human being, but I wouldn't presume he's being driven merely by consuming ambition. I do feel he's a person of intense moral fervor, [who has] a feeling of righteousness. There is the moralistic side of the man. Rizzo is personally outraged, I think, by things such as the Electric Factory. Rizzo has little tolerance for that group of people whose values are so totally different from his. He also is a very intelligent man—certainly no ape or pig as he's caricatured. He's very subtle—the man understands a lot. But his sense of value and temper really make him an intolerant person and he's been in a number of crusades against individuals or people he dislikes."

Before he resigned as a city councilman to run for mayor against Rizzo, even Thacher Longstreth had some praiseworthy comments about the police commissioner:

"I've found him surprisingly sensitive as far as black situations are concerned. I recall one incident in the spring of 1968 when four blacks came into my office and complained of [police] brutality. I took them to the commissioner's office, and he personally interrogated them and ended up by firing one of the officers. I've never seen anyone with the popular acceptance that is given Rizzo. I've been at a meeting attended by members of the press who are not traditionally prone to hero worship. They stood up and cheered when he entered the room. The next night, he attended a meeting of Jewish businessmen and there was almost adulation. At the funeral for a park guard [killed in the summer of 1970] there were women on their hands and knees literally trying to kiss his shoes."

If Rizzo is anything but benign to those he considers the enemies of society, he is equally sympathetic and kind to those he considers "good people" down on their luck. In the spring of 1971, for example, when Rizzo was moving his campaign headquarters from Frank's Collision Service garage in the northern part of the city to the corner of 17th and Chestnut Streets in the heart of the business district, Abie Kanefsky, broke and out of a job, wandered in off the street and volunteered to help clean up the place.

Abie idolized Frank Rizzo. He wore a Rizzo T shirt emblazoned with Rizzo buttons and large letters that carried the message "Rizzo Right Now." Rizzo found out that Abie, forty-five, was once happily married and owned a home in Strawberry Mansion. But his first wife died, his second marriage didn't pan out, and he lost the house when he couldn't meet the mortgage payments.

So Abie was put on the campaign payroll at $100 a week, for which he became a combination errand boy, janitor, and mascot. He slept on a couch in the headquarters until after the election, when Senator Humphrey's campaign workers began moving in. Abie then went to Rizzo and told him he would be out in the streets again unless he found somewhere to go.

Rizzo directed City Managing Director Hillel Levinson and City Solicitor Martin Weinberg to find Abie an apartment, and when they came up with one at $185 a month, Rizzo called the landlord and got the price down to $125.

Rizzo has always held a deep and abiding affection for the "little people," the "guys with the lunch sacks and the oil-stained shirts." Although he himself has a tendency to be pretentious and boastful, he identifies with those who are not.

When he began working out of the Roundhouse, Rizzo frequently had lunch in the cafeteria of Lit Brothers, the least fashionable of the city's major department stores. He liked Lit's roast beef, but he also enjoyed being in the company of the working-class shoppers who frequent the store. As his popularity grew, however, Rizzo had to resign himself to lunch in his office or at a private club, because his appearance in places such as Lit's would touch off near pandemonium, evidence of his tremendous populist appeal.

Occasionally, he would take a walk through the center-city shopping district to talk to the people on the street. Accompanied by several bodyguards, he would move among the shoppers like a famous movie star, shaking hands and signing autographs as throngs of people gathered around him.

To the man on the street, Rizzo was friendly, but reserved; forceful but calm. He spoke with assurance but never shouted and always was polite. To the men who worked with him on a daily basis—his aides and newsmen, for example—this was only one of his many facets. They knew from the inflection in his voice precisely what he wanted and how quickly it was to be done. While he could be earthy and charming, enjoying a good joke or friendly teasing, his mood could change instantly to one of raging anger or vindictive wrath.

News of a particularly heinous crime would unleash him like lava bursting from a volcano. He would leap to his feet, furiously pound his fists on the desk, and swear.

Those close to him also knew that he could be cold and calculating, plotting his move carefully, and waiting until just the right moment to make it. After he became mayor, these were the tactics he used in an attempt to fire Sam Evans, the black man hired by the Bicentennial Corporation to be its executive vice-president at $65,000 a year. But this time they failed.

It says something about the bicentennial bigwigs that they hired Evans in the first place. He had little formal education, and his name was hardly a household word. But the bicentennial leaders hoped his appointment would appease members of the black community who were opposed to the idea of an international exposition in Philadelphia in 1976 because they thought the money might be put to better use.

Until he became personally involved, Rizzo had been annoyed by the whole bicentennial debacle. He was irked by the fact that so many would-be city leaders could not get themselves organized enough even to pick a site for an international exposition. But Evans's contract particularly rankled him.

"Nobody's worth sixty-five thousand a year," Rizzo said. Not, he felt, so long as the mayor only made $40,000. Thus it was only a matter of time until Rizzo went after Evans. He waited for Evans to make the initial move, which he did in January 1972.

Evans, at his first news conference since being hired the previous October, said that the proposed exposition sites in Port Richmond and Byberry—neighborhoods that had rolled up heavy pluralities for Rizzo in both the primary and the election—had to be scuttled because of "racism," "fascism," and "anti-Semitism," on the part of residents in those communities.

What had actually happened was that Rizzo ruled out these sites because he thought a majority of the citizens in the affected neighborhoods were opposed to having an international exposition in their backyards and he wasn't going to "shove it down their throats."

To put it another way, Rizzo already was looking to a second term and these voters were his mainstay.

"I'm going to run Mr. Sam Evans out of the bicentennial,

with or without a contract," he said several hours after Evans made his charges. Evans immediately took off on a ten-day vacation. It seemed inevitable that Evans would be handed his walking papers. But Rizzo had underestimated his foe, who in this case was not Evans but dynamic young John Bunting, head of the city's largest bank, the First Pennsylvania, and the guiding force behind the bicentennial.

Bunting had been doing a slow burn over the fact that Rizzo was usurping his power in the bicentennial planning. The mayor's pronouncements had made it seem that he alone would have the final say about where the international exposition would be held, if indeed it was held at all. The Evans affair quickly brought things to a head. Bunting announced that before any action was taken against Evans, the Bicentennial Corporation would carefully listen to tape recordings of Evans' news conference. In the meantime, he called Rizzo into a private meeting, which, according to several reliable sources, produced a heated exchange of words. Rizzo, after laying out his position, was taken aback when the angered Bunting held his ground with Evans. For one of the few times in his life, Rizzo backed off. He emerged from the meeting to announce that he had "won one and lost one"; meaning that Bunting had agreed to drop the Port Richmond site for an exposition, but that Evans would be retained.

"Nobody gets everything he wants," the mayor said, attempting to save face.

For every setback, however, Rizzo could point to a long string of victories. Among those of which he is most proud was the ouster of School Superintendent Dr. Mark R. Shedd, a nationally recognized educator who had breathed life into the dying Philadelphia school system.

According to Shedd, Rizzo had said on November 17, 1967, the day of the violent confrontation between high-school students and police, that he would "run my ass out of town." Four years later, that pledge became a major plank in Rizzo's campaign platform. And the manner in which he finally sent Shedd packing clearly illustrates his political cunning.

In the spring of 1971, more than a year before Shedd's contract was due to expire, Richardson Dilworth, then school-board president, sensed that Rizzo might be elected mayor, and Dilworth knew that Rizzo would attempt to get rid of Mark Shedd, who, besides being a close friend, he considered to be doing a good job. So Dilworth managed to get the board to pass a resolution extending Shedd's contract to August 31, 1973. This way, even if Shedd were fired, he would leave with a good deal of change in his pocket—an act that only served to heighten Rizzo's animosity toward both of them.

Rizzo could not fire Shedd or even buy up his contract. Only the Board of Education could do that. But the mayor appoints the school-board members, and with the terms of three members scheduled to expire that December and a fourth member due to retire, Shedd's departure was inevitable.

Although Tate was still mayor, he virtually let Rizzo make the appointments, with the expected results. One of those appointed was Philip Davidoff, a career educator who had been demoted by Shedd during an earlier administrative shake-up. The other appointees also were anti-Shedd.

In one of its first orders of business, the newly organized school board bought off Shedd's contract at a cost of approximately $50,000 to the financially strapped city.

Thus Rizzo, in the space of a few weeks, had fulfilled one of his major campaign promises. He had also purged the school board by refusing to reappoint two of its most independent members, one of whom was the Reverend Henry Nichols, who had been acting president since Dilworth's retirement. And he had succeeded in getting elected as the new president of the board one William Ross, a cantankerous old official of the local International Ladies' Garment Workers' Union, a machine Democrat, and a Rizzo supporter.

"This will be a new era in close cooperation between City Hall and the Board of Education," Ross proudly announced.

Men who have worked for Rizzo know him to be a demanding boss. He has boundless energy and he drove himself through many a sixteen- or eighteen-hour day as police commissioner. He expects the same kind of dedication and perseverance from his men.

"It's accurate when people call me a tough taskmaster," he said in an autobiographical sketch published in the *Philadelphia Inquirer*, January 2, 1972. "I have a big job to do and I know I'll never be able to cure all the ills. You won't find ten police who will be critical of me and I was pretty tough on them. But I was fair, too. If you treat people right, they will repay you the same way. I've always had confidence in my ability and I have the ability to lead."

But while he worked his men hard, he also protected them.

"I've dumped more cops than all my predecessors combined," he said. "But if I permitted people with axes to grind and ulterior motives to hurt my men, I'd never be able to look at myself in the mirror—and I have no problems sleeping nights. If there's one thing I'm proud of, it's when I look at the problems other departments are having—the work stoppages, the strikes, the sick calls, the racial problems between black and white officers—we don't have that in Philadelphia. The morale of the men is good and that's one of the biggest factors. They go in on tough calls. They hurry and they're not afraid. That isn't true in other cities."

Rizzo's quick wit has bailed him out of several tight situations. Like the time in December 1971, when he was confronted at a news conference with charges by Dilworth that he had been compiling dossiers on the school-board members.

The charges had been made in a CBS documentary on surveillance that was video-taped in Philadelphia and was to be shown the next night. In an interview with David Schoumacher, Dilworth said: "The police under the commissioner collected dossiers I'd say on thousands of citizens. He has boasted in meetings, one of the meetings with us, that he had as complete files on the people as Mr. J. Edgar Hoover does. At one of our school-board meetings where the mayor insisted the police commissioner be present, toward the end of the meeting the commissioner very ostentatiously threw a number of files on the table and said, 'I've got enough on every one of you . . . to run you out of the city.'"

When asked at a news conference if the comments were true, Rizzo, at first angry, said they were absolutely false and threatened to sue. Then, in characteristic fashion, said he didn't need surveillance on Dilworth. "I've carried him home enough times."

The matter of surveillance was a touchy one for Rizzo. He firmly believed in the need for it. Indeed, the Civil Disobedience Squad compiled dossiers on 18,000 people and more than 600 organizations, mostly during his three-year tenure as commissioner, and the department shared this information with the FBI and other government agencies.

But as Rizzo himself became dovish on the war (he thought that prolonging one that the President had already committed the nation to ending by withdrawal was a waste of human lives and money), he also came to the conclusion that dissenters were not necessarily subversives.

"Unfortunately," Rizzo told Schoumacher, "I agree to some degree that some person at a picket site or a site of a demonstration that the cameras are . . . you know . . . used and we come up with photographs and names of people et cetera, that maybe should not be, and I think that maybe one day they'll have to be a . . . a little homework done and maybe go through the files and remove from the files some of these people who felt strongly against war, who felt strongly against certain things, but by no stretch of the imagination made them a criminal or a suspected criminal or would by any way indicate that they were disloyal to our government."

Of all the charges made against him over the years, the one that hurts him most and the one he hasn't be able to refute successfully is that he is a racist.

"That just isn't true," Rizzo says. "My people were a minority and had a background similar to blacks."

But during the turbulent period of the 1960's, the police—particularly big-city police—became symbols of white oppression in the black community. A policeman became "the man," the uniformed figure who threw them against the wall, searched them, humiliated them, maybe even beat them. The fact that Rizzo was the police commissioner made him the biggest "pig" of all.

Rizzo does not categorically hate black people. He does not consider light skin color a mark of superiority. But he finds it difficult to understand the black ghetto. He cannot relate to its problems, the relationships among the ghetto poor, its image of itself in relation to the outside world, its matriarchal family structure.

He remembers his own father, dirt-poor but hard-working, and he cannot understand black men loitering on street corners. He remembers his mother and the other women in Little Italy scrubbing their steps and sidewalks and he sees no excuse for the squalor of the North Philadelphia ghetto. He remembers having to work from the time he was old enough to push a broom and he cannot tolerate black youths who rove the streets in gangs with nothing constructive to do. He knows what it is to want success and he cannot abide a lack of ambition.

Frank Rizzo thinks of himself not as a racist, but as a man who epitomizes the social values that have come to represent God, Mom, and apple pie. That there is a large minority to whom these same standards represent hypocrisy and intolerance is a fact Rizzo has never quite accepted.

Although Rizzo is a bigger-than-life public figure, his private life—what little time there is for it—is sedate by comparison. Rizzo is not a night-clubber, moviegoer, or much of a socializer. He prefers the company of a few men he feels he can trust. Before he became mayor, Rizzo spent Friday nights at the Vesper Club, a private restaurant and bar in center city, with various politicians and newsmen.

Before the demands of his job became so time-consuming, Rizzo would sneak in an occasional day of hunting. But after becoming deputy commissioner, he found his life divided between police work and his family. There was time for little else.

Rizzo met his wife, the former Carmella Silvestri, through a friend who had taken him to a party in Germantown. They dated for about a year and were married in April 1943. At first they lived with Rizzo's father, Ralph, at his home in Mount Airy. Later, with $1200 given them by Carmella's father, a shoemaker, they bought a small house at Morton Street and Washington Lane.

Rizzo at this time was working at the Midvale-Hempenstall Steel Corporation, where he earned a biweekly salary of $75 as a rigger on a crane.

"Between her father and my father, they helped with the expenses and the bills for the old heater and the leaky roof. With their help, we paid off the $5000 cost in 15 years. In 1953, we moved to our home on Provident Road [in Mount Airy] and have been there ever since."*

The Rizzos raised two children in the two-story red-brick home in Mount Airy. Francis, Jr., twenty-eight, works for the Philadelphia Electric Company and looks very much like his father, only shorter. Joanna, twenty-one, an attractive brunette, was graduated in 1972 from Chestnut Hill College.

According to his brother Joseph, Rizzo was nearly as strict with his own children as his father had been with him and his

---

* *Philadelphia Inquirer*, January 2, 1972. At this writing, Rizzo is building a new home on a six-acre tract in the Roxborough section of the city. According to the building permits, it will cost approximately $125,000.

three brothers. "But he was good to them," Joe said. "He gave them things our father could never have afforded."

Rizzo zealously guards his family and attempts, as much as possible, to keep them out of the limelight. When several newspapers requested that he allow his wife to be interviewed, Rizzo responded by saying that her place was in the kitchen. Several times during campaigns, he did appear with his son, Francis, Jr., and on election night he had the entire family around him. But throughout his long public career, his wife and two children have remained silently in the shadows.

Life at the Rizzo home is light years removed from the constant controversies that swirl around his office. Rizzo will putter around the house or the yard, watch television, read the newspapers, or play with his beloved little Yorkshire terrier, Oliver. He is not much given to parties, preferring the quiet companionship of his immediate family, or the company of a few close friends, or family members who may come to call.

Just after the election Rizzo took his family on a motor trip to visit some relatives in Rhode Island. It was one of the few times in four years he had been out of the city overnight.

Rizzo's dress is as conservative as his politics. He wears tailored white shirts with cuff links and his suits are usually pin-striped, running to dark blue, brown, or gray. He prefers plain-toed black shoes, polished to a mirror glaze, and striped or print ties which only recently have become brightly colored. He is extremely careful to avoid wearing wrinkled clothing, changing shirts two and three times a day. He keeps his fingernails well manicured.

Old photographs of Rizzo show that his hair style hasn't changed over the years. He parts his hair very high on the left side and combs both sides nearly straight back. Despite his age, fifty-two, Rizzo's hair shows only a hint of gray at the temples, prompting rumors that he tints it. Rizzo adamantly denies this, and it is unlikely that he does since he detests make-up and most cosmetics.

On October 14, the night of the only debate between himself and Thacher Longstreth, Rizzo—remembering that Richard Nixon might well have lost the 1960 election because he looked so haggard in the televised debate with John F. Kennedy—allowed a make-up artist at WCAU-TV to powder his face and apply a light eye shadow.

The television people wanted to keep the newsmen out of the dressing rooms, but Rizzo knew his being made up would make a good story.

"Aw, you have to let my friends in," he told one of the ushers. And so reporters stood there joking with Rizzo as Ria Parrish applied the make-up. Al Gaudiosi, his campaign manager, was flabbergasted.

"I can't believe it," he said, shaking his head. "He'll never be made up again, ever. The next time will be when he's dead."

Of all the personality traits exhibited by Rizzo, none is more immediately noticeable than his ability to disarm a critic, to charm the skeptic. Part of it is Rizzo's physical presence—his size, his bulk, and the firmness of his handshake. He walks with a long bouncing gait, legs well apart, and moves with a sense of authority. Aside from the nervous habit of adjusting his clothing, he wastes little motion.

Part of it, too, is Rizzo's ability to take the initiative in conversation, to assert himself and his position immediately. His voice can boom or be quietly persuasive and he can relieve a strained conversation with a witty remark or a clever gesture.

Above all, he is blunt and to the point, preferring the verbal saber to the foil. He seldom parries for position; usually he takes his ground and defends it.

"The guy has fantastic moves," said one of his close associates. "It's hard to get one up on him."

Former Mayor Tate tells one incident that illustrates Rizzo's style. Whitney Young of the National Urban Coalition visited Rizzo at his office in the Roundhouse one day and was impressed by the commissioner's warmth and cordiality. At some point, Young complimented Rizzo on the shirt he was wearing and during the course of the conversation, Rizzo casually inquired Young's shirt size. The next morning, Young answered a knock at his hotel-room door to find a delivery boy with a package from the commissioner. He opened it to find the same brand of custom-made shirt in his exact size.

"That's a great guy," Young told Tate at a later meeting. "He'd give you the shirt off his back."

To his superiors, Rizzo is faultlessly polite. He will address them as "sir," or "mister," or precede their name with the appropriate title.

"He always called me Councilman," Longstreth said.

Always, that is, until he felt himself on an even public keel. When they both were candidates and neither held public office, Longstreth became "Thach." Then, when Longstreth was erroneously dubbed "Fletcher" at a fund-raising dinner in Washington, Rizzo latched on to the same handle. In private conversation he used less flattering terms.

With friends, reporters he trusts, or members of his staff, however, Rizzo prefers first names. He will frequently begin and end each sentence spoken to an individual with the person's first name.

At political or social functions, Rizzo is Mr. Manners. He shakes hands, opens doors, pats children on the head, and keeps up a steady stream of friendly chatter. In his office, he will even empty ashtrays for visitors.

But always beneath the surface lies his volatile temper. Over the years he has learned to control it, but it doesn't take a particularly astute individual to sense his displeasure or realize when a dissonant chord has been struck. Depending on where he is or with whom, Rizzo's reaction to a loaded question or a remark that plucks a sensitive nerve can range from, "That's a little unfair," to, "That bastard said that? Well, let me tell you something about him. . . ."

What it comes down to is that Rizzo defies stereotyping, and this is why so many attempts at profiling his personality have fallen short of the mark. From reading accounts of Rizzo that have made national headlines, it is easy to conjure up images of him as either an Il Duce or an El Cid, depending on one's political point of view. One can find evidence to support either position.

VI

With a Little Help from His Friends

The lead car in the Christmas luncheon motorcade was always a gleaming black Chrysler, driven by Sergeant John Devine. Seated next to him, hand never far from the two-way radio, would be the thick-girthed police commissioner, laughing and relaxed. Two or three reporters—selected each year on a rotating basis—would be in the back seat.

Following the Chrysler would be two or three smaller unmarked police cars, carrying the fifteen or twenty reporters regularly assigned to the Roundhouse, men who, for all practical purposes, resembled policemen themselves.

The motorcade would leave the Roundhouse and weave its way through city traffic until it arrived at the host's favorite restaurant, Old Original Bookbinder's near the Delaware River in Society Hill. With the maître d' excitedly rubbing his hands and waiters flocking near the door, the party would move inside and take up seats at a reserved table.

This event was the annual Christmas dinner Rizzo held for the police reporters, the vanguard of his "team." No notebooks or pens here; the occasion was an off-the-record time for drink, food, and good cheer among friends. Rizzo would pick up the tab.

Soon after he left the department to run for mayor, these loyal chroniclers partially repaid their debt to Rizzo. They presented him with a plaque on which was mounted a $20 gold piece—a token of their appreciation for his having made their lots easier. The plaque is now one of his most prized possessions.

"I get along fine with the news media," Rizzo may tell an inquiring visitor as he displays the trophy. "Look at this. . . ."

"THE WORKING NEWSPAPERMAN made me what I am," Frank Rizzo is fond of saying.

(That, of course, is not exactly the case. There are the considerable matters of his own driving ambition and political cunning. And there were some events over which he had no control, like the time in March 1959 when Mayor Richardson Dilworth called the residents of South Philadelphia "a bunch of greasers." The outcry from that public indiscretion resulted in Rizzo's being appointed an inspector. It was the least Dilworth could do.)

But Rizzo's statement is an accurate assessment of how he won the minds and hearts of most Philadelphians because for more than twenty years, his antics were heralded in headlines and news stories that fill entire file cabinets.

The bulk of these hundreds of thousands of words and pictures grew out of an amazing love affair between Rizzo and the fourth estate. Seldom has a man enraptured so many reporters over such a long period of time.

They vied for his friendship, they consulted him as a father confessor, and they would protect him whenever they could. Along the way, they made him a genuine folk hero.

It all began (not even Rizzo knows the exact date) when he first realized that police reporters were among the most abused and least appreciated men on a newspaper staff. He would see them standing for hours outside a burning building, waiting for a tight-lipped police or fire official to give them some information.

He would observe them in hospital corridors endlessly waiting for an interview with someone whose life had been touched by tragedy. He would look around at the scene of a crime and they would be there, shivering or sweltering in the street, trying to find out what had happened.

Rizzo knew, too, that they had deadlines to meet, incorrigible editors to please, and the job of trying to piece together a story from the most fragmented information when they needed precise details—exact names, ages, addresses, and an accounting of who did what to whom and under what circumstances.

Sometimes police reporters actually assisted police in their work. And once in a while detectives would read in the paper the solution to a case on which they were working.

The reporters did all these things under the most trying of conditions, because the police were often afraid to talk to them. In some instances their superiors strictly forbade them to say anything. And those officials who could talk might refer a reporter to the commissioner, who wasn't always available.

It was a frustrating job, often a thankless one. In far too many instances, these obstacles led to erroneous accounts of a crime. Pressed for time, a police reporter would call in sketchy details from a pay phone. A rewrite man on the other end of the line would piece together the story, embellishing it with fabricated drama and pathos. Police, seeing that the finished product in no way resembled the facts of the case, would blame the police reporter.

Frank Rizzo came up through the ranks at a time when the Philadelphia newspapers gave police and crime stories top priority. A multi-alarm fire was front-page news, a society scandal would stop the presses. So, when Rizzo rode through center city like Sherman through Georgia, there was usually a troop of reporters running after him furiously scribbling notes and frantically searching for the nearest telephone.

Rizzo saw all of this and was smart enough to know that he could use publicity to his advantage. He began talking to newsmen when other officers would shun them. And the police reporters, as well as the city editors, loved him for it.

After he became commissioner, Rizzo took the police reporters under his wing and treated them as if they were his own men. He gave them $35 gold-plated police badges that were as good as keys to the city. Although unofficial, they opened doors. His office was always open to them, too, and they were frequently allowed to sit in it as he went about the business of running the department.

He would take them out to lunch, invite them to his house to play cards, help them out with their personal and financial problems, and defend them if they got in trouble with their editors.

The reporters, in turn, knew a good thing when they saw it and they carefully nurtured Rizzo's image by lauding his accomplishments in their stories. Rizzo's appearance at the scene of an incident sometimes seemed more significant than the incident itself. In October 1969, for example, the *Daily News* ran an eighteen-paragraph story on a peace march. The first fifteen paragraphs were devoted to Rizzo, who had stood in front of the crowd and talked to some of the marchers. The last three paragraphs were given to explaining the nature of the march.

Only upon explicit and rarely issued orders from the editors did police reporters investigate the inner workings of the department and the manner in which its $90-million budget was spent. Police-community relations were largely ignored, as were most of the complaints lodged against the department by citizens.

Instead, the newspapers carried police stories like this one, published in the *Philadelphia Inquirer* on June 6, 1969:

> What was thought at first to be a time bomb was disarmed by Police Commissioner Frank L. Rizzo on Wednesday to the cheers of onlookers after it was taken from a locker at the Trailways Bus Terminal, 13th and Arch Streets.
>
> Exactly what it was never was determined, but when Rizzo disconnected wires leading from a battery to a clock attached to the device, everyone thought it was a home-made bomb.
>
> "God takes care of good policemen," Rizzo remarked with a smile.

Occasionally, Rizzo would be the subject of an analysis piece, perhaps in the admiring vein of one published in the *Inquirer* on November 26, 1967, which began:

> Police Commissioner Frank L. Rizzo has long had the aura of a hero about him.
>
> Big and tough, Rizzo had the presence and the power of the heroes of a thousand Saturday matinees. The good guy, he was fearless in the face of chilling odds, courageous in the continuing battle against those who would exploit, maim and cheat the good burghers of Philadelphia.

Or, in the same manner, this "Man in the News" commentary published on April 16, 1967:

> In the era of the college-boy "New Breed" popularized by television's Sergeant Fridays and the like, he reminds old-timers of the great days of the break-down-the-door-and-lock'em-all-up school of police work. The days of the brick-fisted, choleric, leather-lunged, "copper" who put up with no man's guff and of whom it was often said "you'd better keep out of his way."

The men most responsible for this journalistic charade were the city editors of the three daily newspapers; they usually determined what stories would go into the papers and how they would be written. Rizzo was well aware of this and he went out of his way to befriend them.

But most editors who remembered how the system had worked before he was commissioner were grateful that he had established open lines of communication between the department and the city desks. Thus the newspapers, for the most part, were perfectly content to run police versions of crime stories without making an effort to corroborate and cross-check information with other sources. It was more than they had received in the past.*

So a police reporter in Philadelphia who had been little more than a conduit for relaying information from the police blotter to the city desk was compelled to look upon Frank Rizzo as a godsend. He made their life much easier. An example:

One night in the summer of 1970, minutes after a policeman had been shot, a swarm of reporters and television technicians stood outside a hospital vainly trying to get inside and interview the family of the wounded officer. Blocking their way was a hospital official who refused to budge. Suddenly the big Chrysler pulled up to the emergency room door and out stepped Commissioner Rizzo.

"Let's go in boys," he said to the assembled newsmen. And they swept past the sputtering hospital official.

Net result: the newsmen got their story and Frank Rizzo got his picture in the paper showing him consoling the grieved relatives.

---

* The dangers inherent in this one-dimensional reporting were dramatically illustrated during the Attica prison riot and the Chicago police raid on the Black Panthers' headquarters. In both instances, information attributable to official sources was grossly inaccurate if not intentionally misleading and deceitful. There are countless others that unfold each day with a great deal less notoriety. But the pressures of deadlines and the expediency of printing the "official" or "police" versions of stories have frequently resulted in the newspapers forsaking their traditional attitude of not accepting information—regardless of source—at face value.

With a Little Help from His Friends || 1 2 1

When Philadelphia police reporters were sent out of town to cover a story, Rizzo frequently would call ahead to the local authorities so that the barriers normally confronting out-of-town newsmen could be eliminated.

On one assignment to Wildwood, New Jersey, reporters for the *Daily News* and *Evening Bulletin* were greeted by a police official bearing a case of beer and a sack of sandwiches.

"Commissioner Rizzo called and said to take care of the Philadelphia reporters," the official told the pleasantly surprised newsmen.

If police at the scene of a local incident seemed reluctant to give information to the reporters, Rizzo would soon be on the radio.

"Tell them what they want to know," he yelled angrily on more than one occasion.

Reporters assigned to the Roundhouse found it extremely difficult to avoid being drafted into the Rizzo team. His manner is so patronizing, his personality so persuasive, his arguments so compelling, that to decline his offers required great tact and will power.

Jon Katz of the *Daily News* had been assigned to the Roundhouse for about two months when Rizzo made the first move at gathering him into the fold. Katz, a bachelor, had been living in a small, one-room efficiency apartment on Spruce Street in center city. It was a virtual tomb and he had been fruitlessly pleading with the superintendent of a swanky high rise to be moved up the waiting list of about 300 names.

The day Rizzo got word of Katz's problem the reporter got a telephone call from the building superintendent.

"Do you know who called me?" he asked Katz excitedly. "It was Commissioner Rizzo. Rizzo himself. He said he would appreciate anything I could do to help you. When do you want to move in?"

Katz discreetly declined the offer.

Rizzo's courtship of reporters was not always politically

motivated, however. In most cases, Rizzo is genuinely fond of reporters. He enjoys their company and performs favors for them out of friendship. But even under these conditions, Rizzo expects those to whom he grants privileges or favors to reciprocate by giving him "fair" treatment in their stories. He finds it difficult to understand, for example, how a reporter with whom he was laughing and joking one day could write a story which cast him in an unfavorable light the next.

By the same token, most reporters—even those who sharply disagree with Rizzo philosophically—find him a warm, engaging person.

Trevor Armbrister, a free-lance writer, wrote a 10,000-word story on Rizzo for *The Atlantic Monthly* that was never printed. He said he had a "pretty negative impression" when he first came to Philadelphia to do research for the story in the spring of 1971.

"The Rizzo we see away from Philadelphia is a creature of myths," he said during an interview for *Philadelphia Journalism Review* (November 1971). "I found him more interesting, more human and less of a bogeyman than I expected. I was under the impression that Rizzo was the kind of guy the press clips said he was. But the facts didn't justify that image. I wound up thinking maybe this guy ought to have a chance [at political office]. We liberals haven't done very well in the last four years."

Robert Manning, editor-in-chief of *The Atlantic*, told *PJR* that although Armbrister's article was a "thoroughly professional job," it was killed because it was "too focused on the campaign."

Armbrister, at least, was successful in interviewing Rizzo, which isn't always the case with out-of-town reporters.

Nora Sayre spent two weeks in Philadelphia in 1971 attempting to piece together an article for *Esquire* magazine. She never succeeded in interviewing Rizzo, which was one of the reasons her article never was printed. She found that most politicians and city officials were as closemouthed as the former police commissioner.

In this particular case, Rizzo apparently decided that the publicity would do him more harm than good and he simply avoided it.

Even on the home front, however, Rizzo sometimes had problems with the press.

"I didn't trust him," Rizzo said of Joe McGinniss. "But I took him out to lunch, anyway. I thought he would at least be fair, the son-of-a-bitch. Know what he did? He wrote I told him what to order from the menu. What kind of shit is that?"

What it was, was typical Joe McGinniss, who in 1967 was writing a column for the *Inquirer* and who was the sassiest, most controversial writer in Philadelphia at the time.

Shortly after Rizzo was named police commissioner in 1967, McGinniss wrote a number of columns about him, each one more critical than its predecessor. Rizzo, unaccustomed to a caustic pen, ranted and fumed and finally made his feelings known to the then-publisher of the paper, Walter Annenberg, a close friend of Rizzo's who also had been doing a slow burn in the cloistered sanctuary of his twelfth-floor office.

In a rare, if not unprecedented move, the *Inquirer* published a lead editorial denouncing McGinniss and accusing him of being "determined to make some kind of folk hero out of Spencer Coxe," head of the Philadelphia ACLU and a Rizzo critic.

Nevertheless, McGinniss stayed for another year and a half before resigning to write *The Selling of the President, 1968*, which earned him an enviable reputation and a sizable amount of money. The book must have stung Annenberg all over again, for it was hardly flattering to the man the publisher had so stanchly defended and protected in his newspaper.

Rizzo says he first met Annenberg when his men recovered

the latter's stolen car. Out of this routine police affair grew a deep and lasting friendship. These two remarkably different men truly enjoy each other's company. Annenberg, extremely society conscious and reserved, lives in a different world from Rizzo, the earthy, tough-talking ex-cop. But they frequently dined together and Rizzo occasionally visited the publishing magnate in the *Inquirer* Building.

Just before selling his newspapers and radio and television stations and accepting his ambassadorship to England, Annenberg and Rizzo dined at an Italian restaurant in the Society Hill section of center city. As they entered the restaurant, Rizzo spotted Angelo Bruno, the reputed Philadelphia Mafia kingpin, and several of his lieutenants seated at one of the tables.

"You know who that is?" he asked Annenberg, who responded negatively. "That's Angelo Bruno and some of his men."

Annenberg appeared startled for a moment, and then smiled. "How about that," he said. "This morning I had breakfast with the President. Tonight I have dinner with the Mafia."

Annenberg's philanthropic activities and his close association with Rizzo were in sharp contrast to the style of his father, Moe Annenberg. The empire Walter Annenberg inherited had been built upon a foundation that touched various sources of the underworld.

Moe Annenberg had risen from newsboy to publisher via rough and tumble Chicago in the days of Al Capone and William Randolph Hearst. He became so wealthy that in 1936—at the height of the Depression—he paid $15 million in cash for the *Inquirer*. But his road to riches led through Lewisburg Federal Penitentiary, and he died, many believe, just before he would probably have been murdered.*

* George Murray, *The Madhouse on Madison Street* (Chicago: Follett Publishing Co., 1965), p. 49.

The playing out of Walter Annenberg's nuances and whims in the news columns of the *Inquirer* are legend. He also owned the *Daily News*, WFIL–TV and radio, and *TV Guide*. While Annenberg owned this media empire, Rizzo was protected. But it was with the *Inquirer*, his most expensive toy, that Annenberg played the most. There he manipulated people as recklessly as he jostled type and only a few things remained constant—his unabashed fondness for Rizzo, Richard M. Nixon, and the poor quality of his publication.

In addition to Annenberg there were a handful of editors who were equally attracted to Rizzo, if not more so.

Foremost among these was Harry R. Belinger, who was city editor at the *Inquirer* during most of Rizzo's reign at the police department, and held that same post with the *Daily News* during Rizzo's run for mayor.

Although he worked his way through Temple University by waiting on tables, Belinger never strayed far from the life-style of the blue-collar Kensington neighborhood in which he was born and raised.

Quick-witted, peppery, and conservative, he became one of Rizzo's most loyal friends and stanchest protectors. While he ran the city desk, his paper rarely ran a story critical of the police department or the man who headed it. Even stories that cast the department or Rizzo in questionable light—no matter how objective—would have to carry disclaimers.

In most areas of news coverage, Belinger maintained the skeptical, questioning attitude synonymous with good journalism. For Rizzo and the police department, however, he became an apologist. He would attempt to rationalize the most imprudent action by offering excuses where apparently there were none.

It is enough to say that while Rizzo was unquestionably the most controversial public figure in Philadelphia, while his activities as police commissioner were the subject of heated debate, Belinger was one of his best friends. He became a member of a cabal which met each Friday night at the Vesper Club with Rizzo. After dinner, the two men would sometimes cruise the city in Car One.

Shortly after Annenberg sold the *Inquirer* and *Daily News* to Knight Newspapers, Inc., Belinger accepted the city editorship of the *Daily News* and resigned from the *Inquirer*. He went back to the tabloid he loved—to the fire-engine-chasing journalism on which he thrived.

Rizzo rewards loyalty. Belinger was named to a top post in his cabinet. He became city representative–director of commerce, at $34,000 a year. Remarkably, Belinger was allowed to remain on as city editor for several weeks after being appointed to the Rizzo cabinet. Indeed, the reporter who wrote the story for the *Daily News* stating that Belinger had been named city representative had to wait until Belinger left for the day to get the story past the city desk. And for days after the story ran, Belinger refused to acknowledge to the editor and managing editor whether, in fact, it was true.

Although Belinger was far too close to Rizzo to preserve his objectivity, he made some attempt at concealing his convictions. He never advertised his friendship with Rizzo, and he never purposefully pandered Rizzo to the public—which is more than can be said for the most widely read and provocative newspaper columnist in the city, Tom Fox, of the *Daily News*.

Fox, an irascible conservative, had become enamored of Rizzo during the frustrating years he served as a rewrite man on the city desk. When the Knight chain took over the *Daily News*, the managing editor, J. Ray Hunt, was stripped of his powers and Fox, whose considerable talents had been moldering, was turned loose to roam the city as a columnist. It wasn't long before he beat a path to 8th and Race Streets.

Rizzo could not have gotten better results if he had hired

a top-flight public-relations firm. Fox sang the praises of Rizzo in column after column, carefully tempering tales of the commissioner's toughness with touching vignettes of his kindheartedness, earthy humor, and love for his fellow man.

During the campaign, Fox dubbed Rizzo the "Big Bambino" and became obsessed with the ex-cop's populist appeal. The day Rizzo stepped down as police commissioner, Fox wrote the following:

> There should have been a band there when Frank Rizzo stepped down. There should have been thousands of people outside the building saying to Frank Rizzo that they appreciated what he has done for this town as police commissioner the last four years.
>
> Frank Rizzo is the finest police commissioner this town has ever seen. You anti-Rizzo whifties try biting into that. The man had class and old-fashioned dedication. The taxpayers paid this man something like $29,000 a year to watch over this city and they got a bargain.
>
> Frank Rizzo was the greatest. It has to be said. It must be part of the record. Frank Rizzo is a helluva man. This town may never see his likes again.

A key issue throughout the primary and the mayoralty campaigns was Rizzo's strategy of dodging the issues, the debates, and any neighborhood that might prove unfriendly. Rizzo's aides would privately concede that they had gagged their candidate to save him from himself. But Fox wasn't buying. During the primary he wrote:

> The newspapers in this town are saying that Frank Rizzo isn't talking. They say he is hiding. They say Frank Rizzo is ducking the really big issues of the campaign. They claim Frank Rizzo is not the same forthright fellow he was when he was the police commissioner of this city.
>
> This is a little way out. Frank Rizzo is still talking. If you want to hear Frank Rizzo talk, all you have to do is walk up to him and start a conversation and Frank Rizzo will talk like a radio.

Then, after explaining at length how Rizzo was getting more publicity than his opponents, Fox concluded:

Newspapers usually reserve this kind of ink for assassinations and moon landings and other disasters, but at a time when some people said Frank Rizzo wasn't talking, the *Inquirer* covered him like he was God.

Some people already think Frank Rizzo is God. If the polls hold up, who knows?

Lamenting the fact that the primary had to end, Fox wrote:

The thing that has made the Democratic primary so interesting is the strength of Frank Rizzo. Frank Rizzo, the programmed heavy of the liberals, has dominated the campaign. This is incredible when you stop to think about it because Frank Rizzo's politics is not the sort you would figure to dominate a Democratic primary in a town that is generally regarded as liberal.

The liberals will tell you Frank Rizzo is a ruthless law and order man, an urban Bull Conner. They say he talks too hard. Frank Rizzo does talk hard and when he does he upsets people who paint political rainbows, but here he is leading all candidates in a Democratic primary in a city that gave Jack Kennedy and Lyndon Johnson and Hubert Humphrey majorities that were unreal. You wonder if Democratic politics will ever be the same in this town after Frank Rizzo.

And on election night, Fox wrote:

For Frank Rizzo, it was all one great big anti-climax. Everybody knew Frank Rizzo was going to win this thing. Nobody could have beaten Frank Rizzo in this town. Frank Rizzo is one of those wide, wide-screen bigger-than-life people. Poor Daddy Long Legs was overmatched. He never had a chance.

In August 1970, the city—at Rizzo's urging—turned down a request by promoters to use John F. Kennedy Stadium, home of the annual Army-Navy game, for a major rock concert. Civil libertarians screamed loud and long, but Fox defended Rizzo saying that the Big Bambino, without having to become involved in the "academics of the Constitution," knew that the majority of the people didn't want the concert.

But it didn't die there, as Rizzo had hoped it would. Indeed, it touched off one of Rizzo's most frustrating experiences with the press and marked one of the few times he deliberately exerted his influence to no avail.

Richard Aregood, amusements editor of the *Daily News*, decided that in light of the events surrounding the aborted rock concert, he would use Rizzo's picture as a cover for a rock-music supplement called "The Sounds of Philadelphia." Aregood had an artist put Rizzo in an Uncle Sam suit and hat, with a peace symbol dangling from his neck.

The word got back to Rizzo and he flew into a rage. He considered the picture, without having seen it, a personal affront, an insulting and degrading blow to his integrity, and mainly to his ego. He called a top *Inquirer* executive (the *Inquirer* and *Daily News* had been sold to the Knight chain by then) who tried unsuccessfully to have the cover killed. When it finally ran, Rizzo was surprised that it was not as unflattering as he originally thought. But he still managed to comment, "I'd like to throw Aregood and his goddamned rag in the river."

The acquisition of the *Inquirer* and *Daily News* by the Knight chain came as a blow to Rizzo. He had risen to power with no small amount of help from these two publications. And with the departure of Annenberg for London, he wondered if things would ever be the same again. He didn't have to wait long to find out.

In March 1970, John McMullan, the new executive editor, printed a version of a police shooting that differed from the "official" one released by the police department itself. Rizzo was aghast. He was also very angry, and he had the chief of the Miami police run a check on McMullan, who had come to the *Inquirer* from the *Miami Herald*. He got nothing he could use.

Rolfe Neill, a gregarious young North Carolinian who had

been with the *New York Daily News*, took over the *Daily News*, but he had less immediate success in divesting the tabloid of its interest in Rizzo. Neill hired Harry Belinger away from the *Inquirer* and made him city editor. Belinger, as he had done in the past, rarely ran anything unfavorable to Rizzo or the department.

The *Evening Bulletin* had its share of Rizzo apologists and protectors. Its police reporters operated in the same mirror-of-the-police-blotter fashion as did their counterparts at the *Inquirer* and *Daily News*. Indeed, Albert V. Gaudiosi, one of the *Bulletin*'s top investigative reporters and a Pulitzer Prize winner, became Rizzo's campaign manager.

Of the three newspapers, however, the *Evening Bulletin* far and away gave Philadelphians the most balanced reporting over the years. It ran lengthy series and articles on Rizzo, most notably by Peter Binzen.

Throughout the mayoral primary and campaign of 1971, all three papers followed the policy of giving each candidate equal space, whether or not he deserved it.

Thacher Longstreth set an almost inhuman pace for himself and his staff. He spent as much as fourteen to sixteen hours a day shaking hands, campaigning at subway stops, speaking to neighborhood groups, addressing fund-raising gatherings, walking the streets and introducing himself to the people. He would sometimes arrive home well after midnight and resume the grueling schedule early the next morning.

Rizzo, on an average day, would make some impromptu remarks at one or two fund-raising events in a neighborhood that strongly supported him. The rest of the time he spent in private meetings trying to talk potential campaign contributors out of their money. His total time in actual campaigning before the voters was seldom more than a few hours a day. Yet with rare exceptions he received coverage equal to or exceeding that of his opponents.

This situation was not unique to this campaign nor is it

the exclusive policy of the Philadelphia media. It is the press's widely accepted method of attempting to be fair and it frequently has quite the opposite effect. The equal-space policy assumes that what the various candidates are doing or saying is of equal significance. That, of course, is not always the case.

In this instance, Rizzo spent almost nine months dodging the significant issues, numerous proposals for debate, and dozens of efforts to have him answer legitimate questions posed by concerned citizens and neighborhoods which were less than friendly. Longstreth did just the opposite. He used every ploy short of kidnaping in an effort to get Rizzo into black and liberal neighborhoods. It didn't work. He did manage to confront Rizzo once in what was billed as a debate but which turned out to be a sham. Longstreth carried the campaign into every neighborhood in the city.

What advantages Rizzo gained from the equal-space policy in the news pages were at least partially offset by the drubbing he took from the editorial writers. It was obvious from the outset that most of the media would come out against him editorially. The one surprise was the *Daily News*, which endorsed him but in such a left-handed manner that Rizzo himself wondered where the paper really stood.

"I don't have any quarrel with the working newsman," Rizzo said several times. "It's the editorial writers, the guys who sit in the ivory towers and make judgments when they don't know what they're talking about."

Rizzo maintained that the editorial writers never criticized Longstreth for his "low-road" campaign, his name-calling, innuendoes, and carelessly strewn charges.

"If I had said the things Longstreth said, they would have run me out of town," Rizzo observed.

He wasn't far wrong. The press prayed for the day that Rizzo would "open up," when he would turn on Longstreth as he had turned on the Black Panthers only a year before, daring them into the street for a shoot-out. But he never did, and this proved frustrating to the newsmen and the editorial writers.

Rizzo, too, had his frustrating moments, usually at the hands of national or out-of-town publications. He became suspicious of free-lancers and magazine writers and anyone who worked for *The New York Times*. He had good reason.

The New York Times gave an editorial endorsement to Longstreth even before the campaign got under way. And during the primary, at least one story carried glaring and damaging inaccuracies about Rizzo. But the story that upset him most was an article published by the *Times'* Sunday magazine, titled "The Toughest Cop in America Campaigns for Mayor of Philadelphia."

The article was written by Lenora E. Berson, author of *The Negroes and the Jews*,* a capable writer. But her interest in Rizzo went beyond the scope of a discerning observer. She worked actively with a group of reform Democrats who backed Congressman William J. Green, Jr., in his bid to win the primary against Rizzo. And her husband, Norman Berson, was a Democratic ward leader and state representative who also campaigned against Rizzo.

Her being paid by the *Times* to write an analytical article on Rizzo analogous to hiring Pierre Salinger to write a similar piece on Richard Nixon during the 1960 campaign.

To her credit, or that of her editor, the article was less subjective than it might have been; but it was clear where her sentiments lay, and throughout the lengthy piece she let them seep through.

Since being elected mayor, Rizzo's relationship with the press has changed, in some ways subtly, in others drastically.

The most notable change is in the newsmen themselves. The City Hall correspondents are far less enamored of Rizzo

* New York: Random House, 1971.

than were their colleagues at the Roundhouse. Indeed, some of them hold Rizzo in disdain.

While they welcome the candid manner in which Rizzo confronts them as compared to the hostile attitude of his predecessor, James H. J. Tate, many of them still attempt to keep professional distance between themselves and Rizzo. At the Roundhouse, the reporters vied for Rizzo's affections; at City Hall most of them are more interested in writing good stories. Unfortunately, Rizzo has found it difficult to adjust.

Rizzo is at his best—and he is certainly happiest—when he is holding forth from his office with a group of reporters, preferably off the record. At the Roundhouse, this cordiality gave way to camaraderie, with the result that most police reporters lost their sense of objectivity and skeptical attitude. They became part of the Rizzo "team," his friends and confidants.

This, by and large, has not occurred at City Hall, so when a reporter writes a story or an analysis that is less than flattering or is downright critical, Rizzo feels that he has been attacked personally.

Shortly after Rizzo took office, a reporter wrote that while preaching austerity in government the mayor had increased the size of his personal staff by $100,000 annually; he quickly found himself confronted by a wounded Rizzo.

"He thought I had attacked him personally. He called it a 'cheap shot' to the balls," the reporter said. "I tried to give him a course in journalism and he still didn't understand. In six months, he'll either run me out of his office on sight or I'll have to go to work for him. I don't think there's an in-between."

A further strain on Rizzo's relationship with the press is that he is now being held accountable for an entire city, not just the police department. He had an intimate knowledge of affairs at the Roundhouse. There weren't many questions about law enforcement for which he didn't have a ready-made answer.

But the complexities of big-city government are something else, and Rizzo took over as mayor with less than a working knowledge of the huge bureaucracy. At one of his first press conferences, Rizzo announced that he was going to fire the five members of the board of the Philadelphia Housing Authority. Most of the newsmen dutifully reported what he said.

He was later reminded that as mayor, he could hire and fire only two members of the board, that the city controller appoints two other members and these four appoint the fifth. Rizzo apologized. The papers printed the correction.

As mayor-elect, Rizzo held news conferences daily, usually in the morning. He would discuss plans for his administration and sometimes announce a new appointee to his cabinet.

After officially taking office, however, Rizzo pared these conferences down to once a week, and they became increasingly more formal. Rizzo began scolding reporters for asking questions he thought were unfair. He would refer them to one of his cabinet members if he couldn't answer himself.

Even before taking office, however, he was beginning to feel the heat. He became angry, for example, when a reporter asked him if Belinger was qualified for the job to which Rizzo had appointed him. Rizzo felt personally insulted by the question, charging that it was "unethical and unfair."

Reporters regularly assigned to cover Rizzo find themselves in conflicting positions. On the one hand it is vitally necessary to be liked and trusted by Rizzo in order to communicate with him. He will not be interviewed by reporters he feels have taken a "cheap shot," meaning they have written an article that was critical or hit a particularly sore spot. Members of his staff and cabinet also are loath to do otherwise.

But professional ethics dictate that the reporter should never become so involved with his subject that he cannot approach him objectively. And the reporter, in almost every case, is obliged to write a valid story concerning the subject, regardless of the consequences.

Thus to report effectively on Rizzo is eventually to turn off one's sources of information about Rizzo. To compromise is to risk being beaten by the competing news media and to erode one's professional ethics.

On January 26, less than a month after taking office, Mayor Rizzo agreed to be interviewed by Lou Gordon of the Kaiser Broadcasting System, the man who had, in 1968, trapped potential Presidential candidate George Romney into saying he had been "brainwashed" on the Vietnam War by the Johnson Administration.

The interview with Rizzo was video-taped at the network's Philadelphia affiliate, WKBS. It was scheduled to run ninety minutes. It lasted half an hour.

About twenty minutes into the interview, Gordon produced a copy of *More*, a New York journalism review, and began asking Rizzo questions concerning an article in the publication written by Joe McGinniss. The McGinniss article concerned an investigative piece written for *Philadelphia Magazine* by Greg Walter, formerly of *Life* magazine, which was killed by the magazine's editors because, they said, Walter did not substantiate his charges against Rizzo.

Walter quit *Philadelphia Magazine* and was hired by the *Evening Bulletin,* which likewise refused to print the piece for the same reason. But McGinniss brought out many of the charges in his article for *More*, and when Gordon began questioning Rizzo about them, the mayor coiled like a cobra.

Gordon asked Rizzo if he had pressured the FBI. Did Rizzo report altered crime statistics to the FBI? Did he have files on Richardson Dilworth? Rizzo, becoming increasingly testy, denied everything.

GORDON: Did you have anything to do with killing the story in *Philadelphia Magazine?*

RIZZO: Absolutely not.

GORDON: Joe McGinniss quotes you as saying: "I'm not Hitler, but I'm a tough cop. And if they want to try me, those black bastards, I'll prove it."

RIZZO: I'm sitting here trying to be a pro, but I don't like some of the questions. I've never used that expression. It's unfair for a man of your reputation to throw some of them at me, but I'll sit here and answer them.

GORDON: But Joe McGinniss says . . .

RIZZO: Just because Mr. McGinniss writes it, that don't mean it's true.

The questioning continued and Gordon, sensing Rizzo's rising anger, said: "I won't quote from the article again—I don't think."

RIZZO: If you do, I'm going to leave.

GORDON: The article also said—and this is the last one—that you had received financial support from city night-club owners who are heavily involved in drug traffic and prostitution.

At this point, Rizzo made good on his threat.

"You've been completely unfair," he said rising from his chair. "I'm not going to subject myself any more." With that he walked off the set.

Gordon said he was "sorry that it had to end this way."

The next day Rizzo called Gordon "a garbage collector, a jackal."

The controversy over the Walter article had been raging for weeks. Rizzo repeatedly denied that he had tried to influence the magazine. The magazine's editor, Alan Halpern, upheld Rizzo by saying that responsibility for killing the article was his.

But to the skeptical, the specter of political influence having been exerted seemed very real when, shortly after the article was scrapped, Rizzo named D. Herbert Lipson, the publisher of the magazine, to a blue-ribbon panel to advise him on business and also to the Mayor's Bicentennial Site Selection Committee. Neither position was salaried but both were very prestigious.

Now that he is the mayor, Rizzo will doubtless experience more problems with the press, but he's still exhibiting his amazing ability to impress those assigned to cover him.

On January 24, 1972, Rizzo, accompanied by a contingent of six Philadelphia newsmen, traveled to Washington to meet with Nixon Administration aides on the possibility of channeling more federal money into the city. There were no plans to confer directly with President Nixon, but after meeting a few minutes with John D. Ehrlichman, Nixon's urban adviser, Rizzo was summoned into the Oval Room.

He emerged forty-five minutes later and made the almost unprecedented announcement that the President would meet with the six newsmen. Regular White House correspondents were barred from the meeting.

"In each of the federal programs where there are federal funds available, Philadelphia will get its fair share," Mr. Nixon told them, adding that Ehrlichman had been directed to "personally supervise" all applications for aid from Philadelphia.

"We want the bicentennial city to be well taken care of," the President added.

Responded Rizzo, a Democrat being courted by Democratic candidates in an election year: "He's one of the greatest Presidents the country has ever had."

Later that day came an hour-long meeting with J. Edgar Hoover, and, again, Rizzo got the six reporters and a photographer into the meeting.

"You fellas don't get in here very often, you know," Hoover quipped, acknowledging his legendary reluctance to be interviewed or photographed.

But the times being what they are, and the job of mayor being the almost impossible one it is, the love affair between Rizzo and the fouth estate may become strained, if not shattered. Certainly the stage is set for a showdown between him and the institution that was largely responsible for his rise to power, and it would be ironic indeed if by the end of his term he became, as did Tate, a man embittered at the press, unable to understand why it would criticize, chastise, and attempt to turn public opinion against him.

VII

Of Politics, Primaries, and Soft Pretzels

Frank Rizzo walked out of his campaign headquarters at 17th and Chestnut Streets and into the warm afternoon sunshine. It was May 18, 1971, Primary Election Day in Philadelphia, and he was feeling confident.

As he stood on the sidewalk shaking hands with well-wishers, a car, driven by a Catholic nun, pulled up to a stop. She leaped from the car and ran up to Rizzo.

"Frank, you better win. You better win," she warned. "If you don't, I'll send you the bill for the vigil candles I've burned for you."

Rizzo laughed and quickly replied, "Sister, you better watch your car. You'll get a ticket."

"God," replied the nun, "will take care of my car."

DESPITE REPEATED DENIALS that he would become a candidate in the 1971 Democratic mayoralty primary, Frank Rizzo surprised practically no one when, on February 2, he officially entered the race. For months, newsmen had been aware of his intentions and he privately acknowledged them to close friends and associates. Publicly, however, Rizzo responded to questions about his potential candidacy by saying: "I'm too busy being police commissioner"; or, "I may buy a farm and retire."

So it was somewhat anticlimactic when Rizzo, appearing nervous and fidgety, told a news conference in the auditorium of the Roundhouse that his resignation as police commissioner (a city charter requirement for entering the campaign) would be effective as of 5:01 p.m. that day and that he was no longer a cop but a candidate.

Surrounded by some sixty newsmen and accompanied by his son, Francis, Jr., Rizzo read a four-and-a-half-page statement in which he attempted to dispel many of the criticisms which had been directed at him as commissioner.

"Here and now," he said, "I publicly disavow extremism of the left and extremism of the right. I come as a candidate appealing to the broad middle ground of the electorate. The city lives in troublesome times . . . plagued by problems of drugs, education, housing, employment, and pollution. As police commissioner, I was able to react to these ills in only a limited way. As urban problems mounted, I grew increasingly frustrated. . . . The most direct way to battle these ills is as your next mayor."

During a question-and-answer session following his statement, Rizzo said that he would run in the November election "with or without endorsement of a party."

Rizzo's prepared speech and his responses to newsmen's questions were relatively mild in comparison to the rhetoric he had spouted as police commissioner. The entire statement might have been filed away as just another campaign speech except for a seemingly innocuous two-sentence phrase: "There will be no ducking, dodging, or glib talk from Frank Rizzo. Come Election Day, the voters will know clearly and squarely where I stand on all issues."

That phrase would come to serve as an icy memorial to

Frank Rizzo's silent, low-keyed uncampaign for the Democratic mayoral primary, for, if anything, he left the voters more confused than knowledgeable on just who he really was and what he actually stood for.

Of vital concern to many Philadelphians was the question of who would be running the police department while Frank Rizzo was playing politics. The answer came immediately after he stepped down from the dais. To the front came City Managing Director Fred T. Corleto to announce that Joseph F. O'Neill, forty-six, a steely-eyed chief inspector, would be acting commissioner. O'Neill, who holds a B.A. in sociology, is reticent, and he was virtually unknown at the time. If less a showman than his predecessor, he has since proved to be as tough and as physically fearless.

"People don't realize the seriousness of the Communist threat," O'Neill told one reporter.

Following the news conference, Rizzo's reporter friends hung around long enough to get notes on the commissioner packing to leave. They even followed him as he left the Roundhouse for the last time, many of them with tears in their eyes.

Harry Belinger spoke for many editors when he said that day, "It's just going to make our job a hell of a lot tougher. We never had any trouble getting information when he was commissioner."

The men Rizzo chose to run his primary campaign came from broadly divergent backgrounds, but they shared a feeling of loyalty to their boss that bordered on adoration. His campaign manager, Albert V. Gaudiosi, forty-seven, had been a top investigative reporter for the *Evening Bulletin*. A short man with a loud voice and a quick temper, he was Rizzo's most trusted aide and confidant.

Assisting Gaudiosi in running the day-to-day campaign was Martin Weinberg, the thirty-four-year-old son of late City Councilman Emmanuel Weinberg. Called the "professor" around Rizzo campaign headquarters, Weinberg is a modest man with boyish features. He was a professor of civil and criminal law at Drexel University.

The most influential of Rizzo aides was Norman Denny, fifty, the chairman of the board of Lincoln National Bank, whom Rizzo promised "any top job in my cabinet if I'm elected."

Denny, a transplanted New Yorker, is a member of the Democratic City Policy Committee and the son-in-law of former City Solicitor Frederick Mann. Denny was instrumental in getting the policy committee to endorse Rizzo, despite the fact that the primary was supposed to be "open."

Dr. James Guiffre, the medical director of St. Luke's Hospital, was Rizzo's adviser on narcotics. He had helped Rizzo devise a drug-education program for policemen and had been a close friend of Rizzo's for years. Rizzo frequently refers to him as "my little doctor."

On the periphery of the campaign were several men who, while not directly involved in the everyday machinations of getting the candidate before the voters, played vital supporting roles.

The chief fund raiser was J. Harrison Jones, sixty-eight-year-old chairman of the Continental Bank. Although Jones refused to talk to reporters, Gaudiosi was quoted as saying that "Jones has made enough headway by mid-February 1971 to raise $500,000 for the primary, if necessary."*

And, covering the all-important organized labor front was Anthony Cortigene, manager of the Philadelphia Joint Board, Amalgamated Clothing Workers, and spokesman for 25,000 workers in the city, who is generally considered the most politically powerful labor leader in Philadelphia.

More out of necessity than conviction, Rizzo had been a Republican when he was coming up through the ranks in the 1940s, a period when the city was a bastion of Repub-

* *Philadelphia Inquirer*, February 20, 1971.

licanism. The Democrats finally seized control of City Hall in 1951. Rizzo changed his registration a few months later. But for a brief period, a few weeks prior to his entry into the primary, Rizzo toyed with the idea of running as a Republican. There were compelling reasons for him to do so.

Foremost among them was the fact that the Democratic machine under Mayor James H. J. Tate had been faltering at the polls. In 1969, the Democratic candidates for district attorney and city controller, David Berger and Charles Peruto respectively, had been swamped by incumbent DA Arlen Specter and former basketball star Tom Gola, who had never held public office.

Indeed, Tate himself had barely been re-elected to a second full term in 1967 when he had run against the popular Specter. Tate had won the election by 11,000 votes, and the man who carried him over the top was Frank Rizzo. Specter had combined an appeal to law and order and honest government with a touch of civil libertarianism for what could have been a successful formula in Philadelphia in 1967. But he underestimated the popularity of Frank Rizzo and refused to say whether he would, if elected, reappoint him police commissioner. Tate, on the other hand, was trumpeting Rizzo for all they both were worth.

The results of that election indicated several things: that Tate's personal popularity had all but faded into obscurity, that his ability to lead the organization was practically non-existent, that the organization itself was on the verge of collapse, and perhaps most important, that Frank Rizzo was the hottest piece of political property in town. It was at this point that Rizzo first began giving serious consideration to running for mayor.

Tate, in an era of confrontation politics and social upheaval, was an anachronism. Sullen and insular, he spent a great deal of time talking his way out of corners into which he had painted himself, explaining why yesterday's promise was today's shattered dream, and his credibility gap became a deep and unbridgeable chasm.

In many respects, Tate resembled his counterpart in Chicago, Richard J. Daley. Both men are from Irish-Catholic middle-class families and served their apprenticeships as ward heelers, committeemen, and state legislators. The principal difference was that Tate was never able to run his Democratic organization in the same totalitarian manner as Daley, partly because of some inherent differences in the machinery (Philadelphia, for example, has far fewer patronage positions in city government than does Chicago), but mainly because he lacked Daley's leadership abilities.

Tate came up through the ranks slowly and methodically, as did Daley. He served the party faithfully during its lean years when the Republicans controlled the city, and he had been a state representative, city councilman, council president, and finally mayor. He inherited the mayor's chair when Richardson Dilworth resigned to run for governor.

Dilworth, a colorful man of wit, charm, and intelligence, subsequently lost the gubernatorial election. But Tate, the old-line politician, won election to his first full term in 1963 by 68,000 votes, many of them coming from the machine-controlled black wards in North and West Philadelphia.

Initially, the party hacks were ecstatic over Tate. Under Clark and Dilworth they had been forced to deal with reformist policies. Clark, who later became a U.S. senator, had brought civil service to City Hall, cutting off many patronage jobs that are the vital arteries of any political machine. Dilworth, carrying on the Clark policies, had attempted to extricate the police department from the grasp of ward leaders and committeemen. During Clark and Dilworth's combined twelve years in office, Philadelphia had undergone a physical and spiritual resurgence that did much to make up for the decades of neglect the city had been subjected to under the old Republican machine.

But while the city prospered, the party hacks had been frustrated. Clark and Dilworth frequently acted without consulting them. When Rizzo was using high-handed tactics in raiding the coffeehouses and speakeasies, for example, a number of ward heelers had requested that Dilworth call Rizzo in and have a talk with him; Dilworth refused. With Jim Tate at the helm, however, things like that wouldn't happen. The hacks would be heard and Jim Tate would understand their position because he was one of them.

One of Tate's first political maneuvers was to attempt to get rid of Frank Smith, the Democratic City Committee Chairman who had backed his opponent in the primary, Alexander Hemphill. But Tate failed to muster the necessary two-thirds majority of the party committee. Fortunately for Tate, Smith voluntarily stepped down after the election and slipped into the cemetery for the politically dead, the Board of Revision of Taxes.

Tate, who had won the primary that year with only sixteen of the city's sixty-six ward leaders backing him, wanted to expand his base of power, and he chose as Smith's successor, Congressman William J. Green, Jr. Green was the son of the late William Green, an organizational genius and one of the party's most respected leaders.

Young Green had been named to fill his father's seat in Congress upon the latter's death. Tate had picked the old boss's son more for the Green name than for the son's reputation.

It was a colossal error for Tate. Green, who moved freely in Washington liberal circles, set out to reform the party. He might as well have tried to make the Pennsylvania Railroad a going operation. The ward heelers became embittered and Tate openly warred with Green. Finally, depressed and frustrated, Green resigned the $20,000-a-year leadership post in a huff, saying the party was "closed to the people."

Many wondered why it took him so long to find that out.

As Green's successor, Tate picked State Senator Joseph Scanlon, a capable leader who attempted to heal the wounds of past political in-fighting. He died in 1970, and was succeeded by the man who still runs the party, Peter J. Camiel. A three-term state senator and beer distributor from South Philadelphia, Camiel is a strong backer of Frank Rizzo and has been able to fill the leadership vacuum left by Tate.

Tate suffered another embarrassing setback in the 1970 Democratic gubernatorial primary when he announced his endorsement of State Auditor General Robert Casey, who was running against millionaire-industrialist Milton J. Shapp. Shapp had won the 1966 primary without the backing of Tate and the Philadelphia organization, but he lost the election to Republican Raymond Shafer. In 1970, however, the defeat was clearly Tate's. Casey declined Tate's endorsement; Shapp won the primary and went on to defeat Republican Raymond Broderick in a landslide. All that Tate had to show for the election was a governor who intensely disliked him and another entry in the loss column.

Meanwhile, Camiel, a diligent worker and able politician, had inherited a creaky organization consisting of approximately 10,000 workers, ward leaders, and ward committeemen. About 400 of the committeemen and one of the ward leaders were liberal independents who had defeated organization candidates in the primary. The organization as a whole—having suffered under Tate's bungling and declining popularity—was unwieldy if not recalcitrant.

Thus, as Frank Rizzo readied himself for the 1971 mayor's race, he considered going back to the Republican Party.

"I would have done it, too," he said in an interview on August 31, 1971. "But the Republicans didn't move quickly enough. Camiel and Tate had already contacted me before the Republicans made their move. They wanted me bad, the Republicans. Specter later said so. But I had to make a decision and there it was."

There were other considerations. It was widely accepted, for example, that Green—growing restless under the House seniority system—would also run in the Democratic primary. While some envisioned a bitter split between the liberal and conservative elements, Rizzo was confident he could overwhelm Green in a primary.

But should Rizzo choose to run as a Republican, Green would probably win the Democratic primary and, with machine backing in the general election, would be much more difficult to defeat.

There was also the problem of money. Rizzo listed his total assets at $87,950. He was drawing a police retirement pension from the city of $17,065 annually, hardly enough to help himself finance costly primary and election campaigns. And he knew the Democratic City Committee was prepared to, and did, shell out $130,000 to the committeemen and campaign workers for getting voters to the polls.

It also was virtually certain that Denny, Camiel, and Tate could get Rizzo an endorsement from the Democratic City Policy Committee, thereby throwing the bulk of the organization's power behind Rizzo before the "open" primary was even held.

The Tate problem, however, was a very real one. Rizzo could not afford to shun the mayor's support. At the same time, he had to convince the voters that he was his own man, drawing support from Tate but in no way subject to his whims and orders. It was a tricky maneuver at best and one that Rizzo would have great difficulty performing. Indeed, Rizzo had put himself on the defensive when, on the day he announced his candidacy, he had said, "Several presumed candidates have said they would not appoint me police commissioner if they were elected mayor. Well, the feeling is mutual—I will not serve under any mayor but Jim Tate."

Immediately, Rizzo's detractors accused him of being a Tate puppet. Rizzo bristled and insisted he was his "own man." Privately, he described his relationship with Tate in this manner: "Jim Tate boss me? Never happen. When I was police commissioner and Tate was mayor, who ran the department? Frank Rizzo ran the department. He never told me to do nothing. He kept his hands off because he knew that if he tried to interfere I would quit. So what makes people think he would boss me when I'm boss? Nobody bosses Frank Rizzo. And the people in this city know that."

Finally, Rizzo's decision to remain a Democrat was further enforced by Specter's announcement that he absolutely would not run for mayor again, presumably preferring to wait for a shot at the governorship in the 1974 elections. Specter was far and away the strongest Republican in Philadelphia. Without him—even though the Democrats might be split between Rizzo on the one hand and several other candidates, including Green, on the other—the field looked ripe in November.

The man expected to carry the Republican banner was W. Thacher Longstreth, city councilman and head of the Greater Philadelphia Chamber of Commerce. Longstreth, a tall, Princeton graduate who wears bow-ties and argyle socks, was well known and knowledgeable. But his vulnerable points as a political candidate were all too obvious. His aloof, Ivy-League image made it difficult for the rank-and-file Philadelphia voter to identify with him. That he is somewhat eccentric didn't help either. Longstreth does not wear a topcoat or raincoat, no matter how inclement the weather, and in his home he uses a closet for an office. He was a zealous civic leader, however, a true believer in the city and its potential.

In 1955, Longstreth, then thirty-five, ran for mayor against Richardson Dilworth and was beaten by 132,000 votes. The election said more about the success and popularity of the Democratic reform policies than it did about Longstreth's capabilities.

Since then he has been like a little kid in the classroom waving his hand and yelling, "Me, teacher. Me, teacher." It is safe to say that no man ever wanted to be mayor of Philadelphia more than Thacher Longstreth.

Rizzo was so elated to hear that Longstreth and not Specter would probably be the Republican candidate that he commented, "Thach hasn't got a chance. Know why? He makes telephone calls from his closet and we've found out he doesn't like soft pretzels."

On February 5, three days after Rizzo had announced his candidacy, the first of three other Democratic mayoralty aspirants tossed his hat into the ring. Hardy Williams, thirty-nine, a Negro and a state representative from the Overbrook area of West Philadelphia, officially entered the race. Williams, a lawyer and former basketball player for the University of Pennsylvania, made it clear that he was running for Hardy Williams and not against Frank Rizzo.

"I'm not concerned about him [Rizzo] as a personality or as a candidate," Williams said. "The issues are far deeper than him as a person. I don't have a Rizzo syndrome. . . . I have been called the black candidate. I am a black man. I'm proud of that. Every American ought to be proud of what he is. But let me tell you something else. If, for one moment, you think I'm running in this campaign to be the first black mayor of Philadelphia, forget it. I want to be mayor because I know that I can be productive—with your help—in making Philadelphia a city in which we all can live together fruitfully and productively."

It was precisely this approach that Williams followed throughout the campaign. With hardly any money and no organizational support, he surrounded himself with an enthusiastic group of workers and literally walked through most of the city shaking hands along the way and asking the people to support him. He promised to put an end to the teen-age gang warfare that had claimed more than 100 lives over the past two years. To do this, he told the voters, he would draw from personal experience: he had once been a member of a West Philadelphia street gang.

Rizzo considered Williams more of a curiosity than a threat and, rather than risk alienating black voters, did little more than acknowledge his existence throughout the primary campaign.

For more than a year prior to Rizzo's entry into the race, City Councilman David Cohen, a liberal independent and Democratic leader of the 17th Ward, had been expected to run in the primary. At fifty-six, Cohen, a lawyer, had become anathema to the Tate administration and the Democratic organization. Outspoken and intellectual, he was constantly criticizing the party for its policies on zoning, pollution, and housing. But his favorite target was the police department and the man who ran it. Cohen repeatedly called for the reinstatement of a civilian review board, which Tate, at Rizzo's urging, had disbanded.

While Rizzo held Cohen in utter contempt, he nevertheless welcomed his candidacy. Cohen, it was reasoned, would diminish the strength of Congressman Green, who was expected to enter the race momentarily. Rizzo and his advisers expected the two men would split the liberal vote. Rizzo wasn't likely to get it anyway.

Cohen promoted the most imaginative policies of any of the candidates. He spoke squarely to most of the issues facing Philadelphia voters, but his appeal was limited. For example, his proposal to make all public transportation free and totally subsidized by the city and state fell on deaf ears. Most citizens who did speak out about it in letters to editors of newspapers generally condemned it, not because the idea itself was distasteful to them, but because it had been advanced by Cohen.

Cohen's candidacy seemed futile, and even the news conference he called to announce it on February 25 turned into a shambles.

Cohen read a statement and as he began answering news-men's questions, a bulky man named John Capitolo, chairman of a group known as the Veterans Committee to Support Police and a good friend of Rizzo's, jumped to his feet. He handed Cohen two brown cardboard files which, he said later, contained evidence linking Cohen to Communist causes. Capitolo shouted accusations at Cohen and charged the candidate with refusing to debate him. The news conference that day was a harbinger of things to come.

Then, as expected, William J. Green, Jr., the tall, strikingly handsome thirty-two-year-old congressman, announced his candidacy on March 1. Appearing confident and relaxed, Green told a news conference that he couldn't "sit back and watch the steady decline of the city without doing my utmost to end that decline and infuse this city with new hope and direction."

Although Mayor Tate's influence on the Democratic Party and its candidates was to be one of the chief themes of his campaign, Green made only one reference to it that day. Reflecting on his two years as Democratic City Committee Chairman, he said, ". . . in the end, when my proposals to open and reform the party were turned down because one man's iron grip controlled the machinery of the party, I resigned to fight on independently."

Green was an attractive candidate. Articulate and charismatic, he seemed to have imbibed a Kennedy-like charm rather than having been born with it. A native of Kensington, Green was graduated from Villanova University, where he taught at the Law School until being thrust into politics upon his father's death.

At another time, in another political atmosphere, Green might have pulled it off—maybe in the late 1950s, when law and order wasn't the issue it was in 1971; when Frank Rizzo, if he could have even been a candidate, would have had to deal with issues like civil rights, open housing, and equal education and job opportunities.

But Philadelphians of all walks of life shared at least one emotion in 1971—fear: fear of walking in the streets after dark, of taking a subway, of walking alone at any time. The man who stood to benefit from that fear, the man who the people thought could deal with the sources of that fear, whatever they were, was the swarthy, earthy Italian out of South Philadelphia. Bill Green, as well as anyone, had read and understood that mood. That he forged ahead against such overpowering odds says quite enough about his ego.

On March 4, as expected, Thacher Longstreth received the endorsement of the Republican Candidate Selection Committee and formally announced he would run. In so doing, he resigned his council seat, as required by city charter. Also, he resigned as executive vice-president of the Greater Philadelphia Chamber of Commerce, gave up his real-estate dealings, and also told radio station WIP that he would no longer broadcast the chamber commercials for them. The City Council seat was worth $18,000 a year, his salary with the chamber was $65,000 a year, and no estimate was made of his income from real-estate dealings. In all, the mayor's race cost Longstreth approximately nine months' worth of at least an $83,000 annual income.

Throughout February and early March, Rizzo's profile was ominously low. He had opened his campaign headquarters in the office of Frank's Collision Service.

Later, he moved into a four-story building at 17th and Chestnut Streets in the heart of the downtown shopping district. The building had once been the office of a loan company and the previous fall had served as campaign headquarters for Raymond Broderick, the Republican gubernatorial candidate.

"The place was an absolute wreck when we took it over," a Rizzo worker said. "But look at it now."

Of Politics, Primaries, and Soft Pretzels || 1 5 3

In a short period of time, Rizzo transformed the interior of the building into what could have passed for the central office of a major bank. Because Rizzo's favorite color is blue, the interior—walls, carpeting, and paneled cubicles—was light blue. Sleek new office furniture ran wall to wall, and his aides and workers operated with the same efficiency Rizzo had demanded from the men at the Roundhouse. Papers were piled neatly on desks, the floors were immaculate, the lighting was bright, and Rizzo's office was characteristically plush. It looked like anything but a campaign headquarters.

He had thirty full-time employees and volunteers on his staff as well as scores of telephone solicitors, fund raisers, and mail workers. It was an efficient, precise organization. But Rizzo, the man the city had come to know as an outspoken, ostentatious police commissioner, had suddenly become a political recluse. He wasn't grandstanding for the press, and he dodged efforts at getting him to speak out.

"I am taking my campaign to the people," he would say.

Newsmen in Philadelphia began wringing their hands in frustration. The *Daily News* editorial page repeatedly carried a picture showing Rizzo's face from his nose to his chin, lips tightly sealed. Below the picture ran the headline, "C'mon, Frank. Open Up."

The *Philadelphia Inquirer* published answers to questions asked of the candidates on the front page of several of its editions. Under Rizzo's picture they ran white spaces equal in length to the type under the other candidates' pictures.

WFIL-TV, the ABC affiliate in Philadelphia, had Jim Blocker, host of a local talk show on Sunday afternoons, set up a panel discussion among the would-be mayors. Chairs were provided for all the candidates, and each except Rizzo's was filled. Blocker even provided the invisible candidate a water glass.

The station later issued a public apology.

Finally Green, who was having difficulty getting his campaign off the ground, followed Frank Rizzo to a speaking engagement in the Olney section of North Philadelphia on March 22. When Rizzo concluded his remarks before a street-corner audience, Green seized the platform and publicly challenged Rizzo to a debate. It was a desperate move, one that Green probably wouldn't have made under different circumstances.

Rizzo, however, under the tutelage of Gaudiosi, had learned to keep his political cool.

"I didn't even know he [Green] was here," Rizzo said. "He didn't have the nerve to get on the platform when I was up there. I was already a half block away when he came up. Somebody had to tell me, 'That's Bill Green up there.' He didn't get to say much, though. The crowd jeered and booed. The crowd was with me."*

Later, when asked why Rizzo had repeatedly refused to debate the other candidates, Gaudiosi replied, "My thinking is why inject your opponents into it? Frank talks on the issues. He talks to the people, face to face. Why talk to Green and Cohen and Williams? Those are three votes we'll never get. Frank would rather talk to three women in a playground. He can get their votes."

But that wasn't the whole story. Outside of the affairs of the police department, Rizzo had little working knowledge of city government. His appearances in City Hall were usually limited to an annual trip to council chambers to plead for a larger police budget. And he had never been directly involved in the other areas of municipal operations such as water, sewers, streets, transportation, schools, housing, and welfare.

For that matter, neither had Green. But Green was articulate where Rizzo was harsh-sounding; Cohen had an intimate knowledge of city government; and Hardy Williams was content to walk the streets and talk to the people.

* *Philadelphia Daily News,* March 25, 1971.

It came down to the simple fact that Rizzo had everything to lose and precious little to gain by debating his opponents. Both he and Gaudiosi knew this and acted accordingly. Editors and newsmen also knew it, but while they fitfully criticized Rizzo for not speaking out, they never intimated that it would be detrimental for him to do so. It was one of the reasons why political journalism during the primary campaign was, for the most part, inadequate if not incompetent. Of the three daily newspapers, only the *Daily News* assigned men to each of the candidates. But at least two of them were so prejudiced in favor of Rizzo as to put the objectivity of the paper in question. The *Inquirer,* until the last few days, covered most of the campaign with one reporter.

The highlight of the *Bulletin*'s coverage was its series of feature stories on the candidates' wives. Indeed, at one point, official notice came down from the editors that *Bulletin* columnists were not to write about the campaign or the candidates. The edict was ignored and later rescinded.

After Green's attempt at upstaging Rizzo in Olney, the campaign again fell into the doldrums. But while the press was dutifully reporting that candidate "A" said "B" while speaking at "C," Rizzo was secretly fusing the one bomb he would explode in the primary. Not wanting to make it seem a reaction to Green's challenge in Olney, Rizzo waited more than a week before dropping it.

He chose Palumbo's, a South Philadelphia night club owned by Frank Palumbo, a close friend, as the site. The occasion was a testimonial dinner for City Councilman Edward Cantor. The 500 guests had expected a few patronizing remarks from Rizzo. But stepping before the audience, he said, "You men from the press in the audience better sharpen your pencils, for Frank Rizzo's ready to make some public statements. It's something I want to get off my mind."

Rizzo then alleged that Green, some five months earlier, had approached him in the Vesper Club and said, "I hear you're running for mayor. Let's make a deal. I'll give you forty thousand a year and a four-year contract if you'll do one thing.

"A few weeks before the election, I want you to come out and say you will not serve under my opponent as police commissioner. I know no one can become mayor in this town without your endorsement."

Rizzo then told his stunned audience that there were witnesses to the offer by Green, including Harry Belinger and Councilman William A. Cibotti.

Belinger all but verified the story. He recalled dining at the Vesper Club one evening in the fall of 1970 with Rizzo, Cibotti, and several others.

"In the course of the evening," Belinger told one of his own reporters who was writing the story, "Rizzo and Green huddled with their backs to the table. After the dinner, Rizzo told me off the record that Green offered him a four-year contract at forty thousand a year as police commissioner."

Green was severely stung. The next day he held a brief news conference and labeled the charge "a malicious lie and the act of a desperate man." But his usual calm manner was missing, and he refused to answer some questions on the grounds that they dealt with "divergent issues."

Rizzo followed this up with an "off-the-record" news conference and then said publicly, "I've got some more surprises for the young fella. I've got a couple more of them."

In a prepared statement, Rizzo said, "I am aware of the statement released to the press by Bill Green and wish to re-emphasize and reiterate my statement that Green offered me a deal to support him for mayor. No amount of shadow-boxing or fancy footwork on the part of young Bill will change that fact—that he offered me a deal. It is interesting to note that only one paragraph of Green's eight paragraph statement served as a denial of my statement. And that paragraph shows his supreme arrogance by his failure to honestly face up to my charge. The remainder of Green's press release contains campaign statements which are solely for the purpose of diverting attention from the principal issue—that he offered me a deal."

Tom Fox, the columnist, picked his way through the aftermath and ground out the following:

> You knew it would turn out this way all along. You knew when Frank Rizzo finally decided to talk that he would come on like Walter Winchell. This is Frank Rizzo's style. He hits hard. He shocks people.
>
> He was quiet for so long that some people in this town started calling the former police commissioner Whispering Rizzo. But this is all over now because Frank Rizzo talked the other night at Palumbo's. Frank Rizzo talked in high C's and now young Billy Green knows that he is playing in a fastball league where they throw at your skull.

The voters, meanwhile, were left to decide which of the two men had lied. Most of them believed it was Green.

While the debate over the "deal" raged, it was becoming apparent that Cohen was slipping into a runoff for third place with Hardy Williams. Green was clearly running second to Rizzo, who was far out in front.

Cohen stepped up his attack against Rizzo. Speaking to a group of educators at Thomas Edison High School, in the heart of the North Philadelphia ghetto, he charged Rizzo with covering up organized crime in the city. He said Rizzo "never once" attributed the growing drug problem to organized crime. Cohen was on safe ground here. Several weeks before, Rizzo had made the incredible statement that drug abuse was no worse in Philadelphia in 1971 than it had been in 1961. The newspapers printed the statement without questioning its validity or accuracy. But Rizzo was forced to declare a "war" on drugs when, several weeks after he made his statement, a study released by the district attorney's office showed that drug-related deaths in 1970 were greater than traffic fatalities.

Several FBI reports had named Angelo Bruno of South Philadelphia as the head of a Mafia family that controlled organized crime in Philadelphia and southern New Jersey. Cohen accused Rizzo of maintaining a hands-off policy regarding Bruno, who at the time was in the Yardville, New Jersey, penitentiary for refusing to answer questions posed by the New Jersey State Commission of Investigation.

"Is it that you are covering up for organized crime?" Cohen challenged. "Is that what you and Angelo Bruno talked about when he visited you just after you were appointed commissioner? It's time to come clean and tell the people why you always threaten the addicts and the judges but never the big men behind the drug traffic."

Two weeks later, still campaigning among the black neighborhoods of North Philadelphia, Cohen said Rizzo "represents a Frankenstein for Philadelphia. I'm raising my voice against Jim Tate and Frank Rizzo as evils that have to be excised from Philadelphia. They are cancerous growths that require radical surgery. The surgery is required to remove Frank Rizzo, who is a stooge and a tool for Jim Tate."

Cohen then made a charge that was to capture the headlines for several days.

"Frank Rizzo in the summer of 1965, when he was deputy police commissioner, personally clubbed down young people seeking to open the exclusive policies of Girard College. Frank Rizzo personally led the clubbing because he does not understand freedom of dissent, opinion, or legitimate opposition. He was promoted for his fine work less than two years later. There was nothing done about that incident because it was referred to the Police Advisory Board, but the secretary of that board was a deep friend of Rizzo's, Clarence Farmer [head of the city's Human Relations Commission]."

Rizzo denied the charges and Cohen later reiterated them. To help clear up the matter, WHYY-TV, the public educational-television station, set up a private screening of films of the incident for the news media. The films did not substantiate Cohen's charges, although they showed Rizzo and several other cops dragging a student behind a car, billy clubs in hand. The student was beaten, but the films failed to show who administered the blows.

Cohen's candidacy, however, was not enhanced by the ploy. Cohen could hurt Green, but not Rizzo. He could also draw votes from Hardy Williams, who, in turn, could siphon off strength from both of them. What it came down to was that Rizzo had a strong following that could not be swayed against him, no matter what evidence might be brought before them. The other three men could divide the anti-Rizzo vote among themselves. The only possibility of defeating Rizzo was to unite behind one of the other candidates, preferably Green. And even that might not be enough. Cohen would come to realize this far too late in the campaign.

On April 21, national pollster Oliver Quayle, accompanied by syndicated columnists Rowland Evans and Robert Novak, spent a day feeling the pulse of the Philadelphia voter. The results substantiated Rizzo's overwhelming popularity:

> Fully 83 percent of the 60 registered Democratic voters we sampled in three wards in Philadelphia gave Rizzo a job performance of "excellent" or "good" during his tenure as police boss.
>
> And yet, among blacks alone, who comprised 30 percent of our survey, Rizzo got a strong 60 percent positive ("excellent" or "good") rating. With whites he scores an amazing 93 percent.
>
> With the undecided distributed proportionately, we found Rizzo with 51 percent of the primary vote; Green 33 percent; State Rep. Hardy Williams, the only black candidate, 8 percent; and former City Councilman David Cohen, 8 percent. Thus, even if the three liberal candidates—Green, Williams,

and Cohen—should join forces behind Green, Rizzo looks almost unbeatable as of today.

Thus only one stumbling block stands between Rizzo and a stunning triumph in the May 18 primary and next November's general election. That is the concern we detected among several voters that although he was a great police commissioner, he lacks the political poise and polish to be mayor.

That hazard seems pale, however, against the pervasive power of the law and order issue. . . .*

Green, realizing that he was in deep trouble, began calling on national Democratic Party leaders to assist his faltering campaign. Among them was former United States Attorney General Ramsey Clark, who spoke on behalf of the congressman at a lawyers' reception at the Art Alliance.

"We never had to worry about where he [Green] stood on civil rights, effective crime control, and the problems of our cities," Clark said. In obvious reference to Rizzo, Clark, speaking on drugs, added, "The police stick never cured an addict, you can't beat heroin out of the blood of a human being."

Rizzo failed to follow up on his other "surprises" for Green and continued a lazy schedule of one or two fund-raising speaking engagements a day. He became a man for all constituencies, his speeches and statements running from politely middle of the road to knee-jerk right wing. Before an informed citizens' group, he would speak of such issues as drug abuse, crime, and how to attract new industry to the city. On other occasions, when his audience was largely working-class white, he would be reminiscent of George Wallace.

At one fund-raising dinner in the northeast section of Philadelphia, an almost all-white, middle-class section of the city, heavyweight champion Joe Frazier made a surprise appearance and endorsed Rizzo for mayor. Ironically, Frazier—although usually said to be a resident of Philadelphia, he

* *Philadelphia Inquirer*, April 22, 1971.

actually lived in neighboring Montgomery County—wasn't eligible to vote in the Democratic primary. Rizzo used the occasion to make this statement:

"I wouldn't have gotten into the race if they had come up with the right name or the right candidate. But I couldn't let this city fall into the hands of the lefties."

With less than two weeks remaining before the voters took to the polls, four events occurred that transformed the sometimes slapstick primary into a comedy of errors.

On May 6, David Cohen suddenly quit campaigning in the streets, walked into a news conference, and announced he was dropping out of the race to support Green. Even some of his closest associates were surprised by the announcement. Later, the two men held a news conference and with tears in their eyes, Green told newsmen and campaign workers, "This is the most extraordinary act of political courage I have ever seen."

It was also an act that saved Cohen from suffering a most embarrassing defeat. Rizzo, of course, wasted no time in analyzing the situation.

"It proves that Green, who gives lip service to antibossism, has finally found someone with whom he can make a deal."

Green, however, was exhilarated.

"I rolled a seven. And tomorrow I am going to roll an eleven."

The next afternoon, Governor Milton J. Shapp endorsed Green.

"I have tried to maintain my neutrality," the governor said. "But it is now apparent that the Democratic voters of Philadelphia must make a fundamental choice between the forces of hope and the forces of fear. For the future of this city and for the progress of Pennsylvania, Philadelphia must have a mayor who is progressive, enlightened, independent, and compassionate . . . a man who will protect the vital interest of all its people. But there are other reasons why I have become involved in this election. I am disappointed by the campaign of Mr. Rizzo. I am disappointed that he failed to respond to the legitimate question raised by the press and other concerned groups who wanted to know where he stood on the issues. I am distressed at his failure to testify before City Council on the pressing financial problems of the city. I am also deeply concerned by the rise in drug traffic, the increase in the crime rate, and the epidemic of gang killing which occurred while he was police commissioner. Mr. Rizzo's nomination would not encourage the forces of hope or increase protection afforded to Philadelphia citizens. His election would be a severe blow to the need in Philadelphia and Pennsylvania, and, indeed, for the entire nation, for a just and decent society."

Shapp's endorsement of Green not only contradicted several statements in which he said he would not become involved in the primary, but it was detrimental to his own best interests as a governor seeking to put through a legislative package for which he would need the support of Philadelphia's Democratic delegation.

On February 4, for example, just weeks after he assumed office, Shapp said, "No members of my staff will be permitted to work for any candidates in Philadelphia or any local elections throughout the state. I have enough problems in Harrisburg without getting involved in the mayoralty race."

Referring to Rizzo's candidacy, the governor said, "Rizzo is a citizen of Philadelphia and has as much right to run for office as I had to run for governor."

On March 26, Shapp made this statement: "I am taking no position in any of the primaries anywhere in the state. My job as governor is not to interfere with the democratic process of selecting the candidates. Open primaries are beneficial to the party and the people. I'm delighted to see so many candidates running this year."

Also, there appeared to be a resentment on the part of the voters to "outsiders" becoming involved in a local election. Clark's appearance on behalf of Green had no positive effect. Nor had similar appearances by Senator Edward M. Kennedy and former Ambassador Averell Harriman. To the contrary, Philadelphia in the spring of 1971 was strongly conservative in mood and, if anything, Green's SOS to the liberal wing of the national Democratic Party had probably damaged his chances of winning the primary.

As a spin-off of Shapp's endorsement came the announcement by State Attorney General J. Shane Creamer that his office would investigate the charges of brutality lodged against Rizzo by Cohen. The move was so political as to be ludicrous. The statute of limitations having already been exceeded, Creamer came under stiff criticism from the news media. But it stunned Rizzo nevertheless.

In a private interview after the primary, he said that the Creamer incident had hurt him "personally."

"I worked very closely with him when he was a lawyer and I was the commissioner," Rizzo said. "I had a good crime library at the Roundhouse. Once he told me he was having trouble finding two books he needed and asked me if I had them. I checked my library and found that I didn't. So I bought them out of my pocket. Cost me twenty-nine dollars. I sent them to him as a gift. We were that close. Then the son-of-a-bitch turns right around and pulls a stunt like that. It hurts, I tell you, things like that hurt."

Publicly, he had this to say about Shapp: "You have seen a governor prostitute himself. You'll notice that Governor Shapp's timing was off. I'm not a politician. But I'm beginning to feel like a politician. I'm getting to enjoy this campaign. My opponents are coming at me like jackals."

But these issues were pre-empted on May 11, when the *Daily News* published a poll showing Green running a poor third behind Rizzo and a full 7 percentage points behind Hardy Williams.

The poll was conducted by a local firm called Associates for Research in Behavior, Inc., which had no experience in political polling. The results showed Rizzo with 30 per cent of the vote, Williams with 19 per cent, Green with 12 per cent, and 33 per cent of the voters still undecided. It also gave Cohen 6 per cent, since it had been conducted prior to his dropping out of the race.

The results alone were enough to raise doubts about the validity of the poll. Williams had never been considered a strong contender. The Quayle poll; Green's own pollster, Harry Rivkin; and polls conducted by Rizzo all showed Green running second to the former commissioner.

Beyond this were several basic flaws in the way it had been taken. Only 157 voters had been sampled. Only 30 locations in the city had been polled. There was some question as to whether the sampling had been made at random. And it was thought that too many blacks had been questioned.

Green immediately charged into the offices of *Daily News* Editor Rolfe Neill the day the poll's results were published on the paper's front page. He said the poll not only was inaccurate, which it was, but he said it had hurt his chances of pulling in the undecided voters and had dried up many sources of campaign financing. He made his case. On Tuesday, the day after the results were published, the paper ran Green's criticisms. On Wednesday, the *Daily News* ran an editorial signed by Neill that covered half the front page of the afternoon tabloid:

Congressman William Green challenges the methodology of this poll. After investigating his complaints, I have reasonable doubt about the accuracy of the poll information concerning Green and Hardy Williams. We should have said when we published the poll that the pollster's 157 interviews have a plus or minus error factor of 7½ percent. For example, a candidate who showed 30 percent of the votes could receive as much as 37½ percent or as little as 22½ percent. The probability of error is present in all polls. The larger the sample the smaller the chance of error. On 400 interviews, for instance, the plus or minus factor is just over 3 percent. The democratic process is both precious and fragile. This newspaper seeks to enhance that process, not interfere with it. I believe the doubtful poll information we printed ranking Green and Williams has probably been used to harm Green's campaign. My apologies to Congressman Green for that. Secondly, my apologies to our readers. Beyond this what do we intend to do? We will present a final political poll on Monday, the day before election. As always, it will be paid for exclusively by the *Daily News* and be independent of any party or candidate.

Neill was criticized for his lack of foresight in publishing the poll, but was also praised for his courage in openly admitting his error on the front page. "But you can only do that one time," he said.

As promised, the *Daily News* came back the following Monday, the day before the primary vote, with what it headlined:

THE POLL
It's Rizzo; Then Green, Williams
But 30% of Democrats Undecided

The results gave Rizzo 32.2 per cent of the vote, Green 23.7 per cent, Williams 14.1 per cent, and 30 per cent undecided. "*THE* POLL" had been conducted by Chilton Research Services, which sampled 590 registered Democrats during a three-day telephone survey. The pollsters said it had an error factor of 3.8 per cent.

The poll was accepted as being accurate—except by Rivkin, who maintained that Rizzo and his employer were neck and neck, with the undecided vote the determining factor. Rizzo, meanwhile, was saying his polls placed him well out in front with more than 50 per cent of the vote.

Tuesday, May 18, was a beautiful spring day. The sun beamed through a virtually unpolluted sky and the temperature hovered in the seventies. It is usually a fact that a heavy primary vote generally runs against the organization of power, and seldom do primaries in Philadelphia turn out 50 per cent of the registered voters. But on this Tuesday a record 65 per cent of registered Democrats (many Republicans had switched over so they could participate) came to the polls. Rizzo won it walking away.

The final count in the 66 wards and 1753 voting divisions gave Rizzo 176,621; Green 127,902; Williams 45,930; Cohen (who had stepped down too late to have his name taken off the ballot) 4176; and 11,930 went to a mixed bag of unknown candidates.

Rizzo had fallen 8267 votes short of a majority. But he had gotten more votes than Green and Williams combined. Rizzo had carried 37 wards, Green 26, and Williams 3. The latter's poor showing in the black wards, most of which went to Green was surprising. Williams carried his own ward—the 3rd—in the Overbrook section of West Philadelphia, and two wards, the 14th and 20th, in North Philadelphia.

Rizzo's big pluralities, as expected, came from his native South Philadelphia, where he carried five predominantly Italian wards by 25,000 votes—more than half his margin of victory over Green. He also carried the white working-class wards in Kensington and Frankford, and swept the entire sprawling northeast section of the city.

Green lost his own ward, the 23rd, to Rizzo and, in fact, Rizzo won eight of fourteen wards in Green's Congressional district. Green's strength came from predominantly black West Philadelphia center city, and the white, upper-income areas of Germantown, Mount Airy, Chestnut Hill, and Wynnefield.

Rizzo won the primary by fewer votes than had Tate in 1967, when he defeated Alexander Hemphill by 71,000 votes. But Rizzo won big despite the fact that the Democratic coalition fused by Congressman Green's father had been split wide open. Since 1951, the Democratic organization had always scored heavily in the black wards. Green and Williams took the vast majority of this vote.

On the Republican side, Thacher Longstreth won a lopsided victory over a slew of nonentities. He polled 90,413 votes—less than the 100,000 votes that Republican Party City Chairman William J. Devlin had hoped for, and the total vote had fallen short of his anticipated 30 per cent.

The Republicans also were alarmed by the fact that more than 17,245 voters had switched registration from Republican to Democrat. Also, Rizzo had drawn heavily from the nominally Republican Jewish wards in northeast Philadelphia and from three South Philadelphia wards—the 26th, 39th, and 48th—that usually voted with the GOP.

The Republicans could only be thankful that the Democratic Party seemed split. Their sole hope was that Green, Williams, and Cohen would campaign against Rizzo in the general election.

They seemed to forget that Green had lost his own Congressional district and would be up for re-election in 1972. Indeed his Congressional district later was combined with that of Congressman James A. Byrne. Green, however, won the primary fight and Byrne was forced to retire from Congress after holding a seat for twenty years.

For Frank Rizzo it was a clear victory. He left for a vacation in New England, and Gaudiosi went to Tate's summer home in the shore community of Longport, New Jersey.

They would face Thacher Longstreth and beat him in November. Because, after all, how could a man who didn't like soft pretzels be elected mayor?

VIII

The Uncampaign

On a Sunday in July, long before either candidate should
even have thought about taking to the stump, Longstreth
started it. And, of all places, at the South Jersey shore.

As thousands of Philadelphia row-house dwellers relaxed
on the brown sand and broken clam shells, a biplane,
looking for all the world as if it had just flown off the set
of *The Blue Max*, appeared on the horizon.

It swung in parallel to the beach and leveled off at about
five-hundred-feet altitude. Just another one of those aerial
advertisements for salt-water taffy—or was it?

Suddenly people started pointing and mumbling. Heads
peeked out from under cabañas. Frisbees flopped onto the
sand. There, trailing the sputtering biplane by fifty feet or
more, standing out in blazing red letters against the cloud-
less blue sky, was the opening shot of the campaign:

RIZZO IS A BULLY

IT TOOK TEN MONTHS and more than a million dollars
to put Frank Lazzaro Rizzo in the plushest office on the
sixteenth floor of the Municipal Services Building. It was the

longest, costliest mayoral campaign in Philadelphia's history.

Rizzo's staff used a forest of paper as they ground out press releases and position papers. There were hundreds of fund-raising activities, and tons of roast beef and mountains of green peas were consumed.

There were Rizzo hats, Rizzo buttons, Rizzo bumper stickers, and Rizzo T shirts. There was a South Philadelphia fife and drum corps that played almost everywhere he went. There were even Rizzo Girls in bright-red hot-pants.

No matter where you looked in Philadelphia, there was something to remind you that Frank Rizzo was a candidate for mayor. On the sides of public buses. In subway concourses. On newsstands. On taxicabs. On gigantic billboards at strategic locations throughout the city.

More than $80,000 was spent on advertising during the last two weeks of the campaign. Radio stations continually blared Rizzo spot ads. Television carried thirty-second advertisements that cost $1500 each. Rizzo himself put the pinch on practically everyone he knew, and a few of the most loyal invested $1500 in Frank Rizzo wristwatches.

Even if all this were somehow missed, a Philadelphian could get the message from men who prowled the city in cars and extolled the virtues of Rizzo by bullhorn or public-address system. They could also get it from the battalion of telephone volunteers or the squads of workers who passed out pamphlets.

His staff worked relentlessly, tirelessly. It was as if they were listening to the nonstop strains of "Happy Days Are Here Again." But it was more than euphoria that drove them. They remembered how the Democrats had almost lost the last election when they had an albatross in the form of James Hugh Joseph Tate heading the ticket. To a man and a woman, they exuded confidence, a bubbling enthusiasm that never waned. They pulled out all the stops. They left not a stone unturned. Except maybe for one—the stone their candidate seemed to be hiding under.

In spite of all the hoopla and the cornflakes, the schlock and the spiel, Rizzo for most of those ten months was an invisible candidate with a muted voice. He came very close to running a campaign by proxy.

At the other extreme was his opponent, six feet six inches of nervous energy named W. Thacher Longstreth, who, despite a schedule that should have hospitalized him, managed to sneak away to Princeton, New Jersey, every fall weekend that his beloved Tigers played a home game.

Longstreth's blood line is etched across the pages of Philadelphia history all the way back to the ship that brought William Penn to the banks of the Delaware in the late seventeenth century. His forefathers, strict Quakers, had fared well until the Great Crash in 1929, when Thacher was left to work his way through Haverford School, winning a scholarship to Princeton, where he was a track star and an honorable mention All-American football end. He was elected president of his senior class and voted its best all-around man.

Longstreth faked his way through an eye examination to join the Navy and after being discharged became an advertising salesman for *Life* magazine in Detroit. In 1950, he came back to Philadelphia and several jobs with local advertising agencies. His first venture in politics was as astoundingly unsuccessful as would be his latest: he worked for Wendell Willkie.

To the man on the street, Longstreth looked as if he hadn't changed a bit since he toted books around the Princeton campus. Even the clothes draped around his thin frame appeared the same—tweed sportcoats and cuffed pants, thick soled oxford shoes, white or blue button-down shirts, and bow ties. And, of course, his trademark, the argyle socks.

"All kinds of efforts have been made to get me to abandon my socks. Well, I've worn my socks all my life. What the hell, I'm not going to change them now," he said. Indeed, he tried to use them to his advantage. Once at a rally during the campaign, he hiked up one pants leg, propped his foot up on the edge of the stage, and broke into several verses of "Love Is Lovelier the Second Time Around."

Some were amused, or at least confused, by Longstreth. At times his boyish enthusiasm and his naïveté made his candidacy seem almost whimsical. Who but Longstreth, for example, would tell Rizzo on the night the latter won the Democratic primary: "You smote 'em a mighty blow."

But by the time it was all over, everyone knew this bow-tied Ivy Leaguer had been in the race.

While Rizzo spent most of his time trying to get contributors to pull their wallets out of their pockets, Longstreth was getting people to pull their hands out of their pockets. He shook more than 100,000 of them and traveled more than 16,000 miles within the city limits to do it.

"Hi," he would say, grinning ear to ear, "I'm Thacher Longstreth. Glad to meet you." And he would stand there and make small talk, his bow tie bobbing with his Adam's apple. Longstreth was in every neighborhood. Every Sunday he delivered a guest sermon in a different church. He hit the concourses and the elevated stops and walked the downtown streets, his obsession to be mayor driving him past the point of fatigue and frustration.

So, from the very beginning, from the day that rickety old biplane passed above the sweltering throngs at the shore, the pattern of the fight was set. Longstreth would take it to his opponent. Rizzo would stay in his corner except for one round—a round Longstreth would lose. The rest of the long, dreary, bitter campaign would be a display of shadow-boxing by the man who had the reach but not the knockout punch. Rizzo would win it by a decision, although not an overwhelming one: 394,067 to 345,912.

To put it another way, you can't whip a man who won't fight.

The Rizzo election strategy was merely an extension of his primary strategy. From the results of that first race it was obvious that the old voting patterns would not hold up. The black vote, which had been cultivated and harvested by the Democratic ward leaders and committeemen since the 1930s, was going to bolt this time out because, justly or unjustly, Rizzo was poison in North and West Philadelphia.

So he ignored the black wards, making only infrequent unannounced stops at fund-raising functions. There were two reasons for this approach. First, anything else would be a waste of time. No amount of talking or cajoling would significantly alter his poor primary showing in the twenty-two of the city's sixty-six wards where the population is more than 50-per-cent black. Rizzo had carried only 24 per cent of the vote in these wards in the primary and had won only one of them, the 36th in South Philadelphia, the domain of Congressman William A. Barrett, an efficient vote-getter and an old-line party stalwart. Why, it was reasoned, waste time and money?

Second, and most important, Rizzo and his strategists knew that if he campaigned in the black wards, there would surely be demonstrations against him. There might even be violence, and that would be a catastrophe. He wasn't about to give Longstreth living proof of what the latter had been saying all along—that Rizzo was the white candidate.

To offset the loss of this sizable block of nominally Democratic votes, Rizzo could count on carrying by large majorities the heavily populated, predominantly Italian wards in South Philadelphia, which traditionally vote Republican. To this could be added the white working-class wards in Kensington, Fishtown, and Port Richmond along the Delaware River, and also southwest Philadelphia.

With Longstreth virtually assured of carrying Germantown, Chestnut Hill, Mount Airy, center city, and North and West Philadelphia, the election would be decided in the great northeast, some twenty-two wards of mostly white middle-class and Jewish voters.

Rizzo had carried every one of these wards in the primary. He needed a repeat performance to win the election.

By the same token, Longstreth also needed to carry the northeast or at least run well enough to offset Rizzo's expected bonanza in South Philadelphia.

The problem for Longstreth was at once uncomplicated and unsolvable. He had to run against Rizzo, not for himself. Somehow he had to puncture the Rizzo myth, to peel off the veneer of his legend, and expose the man beneath it. In effect, he had about six months to remake the image that Rizzo had carefully molded for more than two decades.

Rizzo's campaign trail would run almost a straight line between South Philadelphia and the northeast, with stops along the way in Frankford, Kensington, Fishtown, and Port Richmond. Longstreth would move like a kinged checker, hopscotching into every neighborhood in the city.

The two men who plotted the campaign for the candidates were both forty-seven, intelligent, hard-driving natives of West Philadelphia. They even resembled each other physically—short, heavy-set, and conservatively dressed. But the similarities ended there.

Rizzo's campaign manager was Albert V. Gaudiosi, tough-talking and intense, with a temper as explosive as Rizzo's, and he displayed the same style of street-smart cunning. Gaudiosi is very close to Rizzo. The two had become friends back in the mid-1960s, and as the campaign moved along, it became obvious that Gaudiosi, more than invoking Rizzo's absolute trust, began making many of the major decisions. There were many times when Rizzo's gut instinct was to lash out at Longstreth, but Gaudiosi managed to hold his candidate in check. When Rizzo did open up, it was never with the full venom and fire of which he is capable. Rizzo observers could recall no man who had more influence on him than did Gaudiosi.

If Gaudiosi reflected the mannerisms of Rizzo, so also Clifford Brenner mirrored the style of Thacher Longstreth. Brenner, urbane and soft-spoken, is a graduate of Penn State University. After brief stints at the *Inquirer* and *Bulletin* as a reporter, he joined Richardson Dilworth's mayoral campaign in 1956. When Dilworth became president of the Board of Education in 1966, he hired Brenner as a special assistant. While working in that position Brenner developed the nationally known "Parkway Project," an innovative "high school without walls." More recently he had been a partner in a prominent advertising–public relations firm.

Both men were well versed in city politics, although their approaches differed. Brenner is considered an idea man whereas Gaudiosi is generally thought of as being shrewd and calculating. But each was confident his respective man would win. For Brenner, it was playing catch-up. For Gaudiosi, it was attempting to maintain a lead that at first was overwhelming, but one that would surely diminish as the campaign rolled along.

If the long and usually bitter campaign was uninformative, it was not without humor. On September 16, for example, Longstreth took his campaign to Washington, D.C., for a fund-raising cocktail party at the Sheraton-Carlton Hotel. It was sponsored by a bipartisan committee headed by Mrs. C. Grove Smith, the daughter of F. Scott Fitzgerald. More than 300 prominent liberals and their ladies showed up, among them Senator Jacob K. Javits of New York, former Attorney General Ramsey Clark, Senator Eugene J. McCarthy, and Republican Senator Richard S. Schweiker of Pennsylvania. It was all smiles and drinks and well-wishes.

McCarthy likened Rizzo's campaign to the Vietnam War, saying, "There must be another way to obtain peace in the nation's cities. Physical strength is not the answer. There must be another answer, but I know it is not going to be easy."

McCarthy may not have known the answer but Javits and Clark didn't even know the name of the man they were applauding.

"Fletcher" Longstreth, they called him and Rizzo later quipped: "Those bastards didn't even know his name."

The incident, however, underscored a major problem for Longstreth. He was suffering from an identity crisis. Despite the fact that he had run for mayor once before, had served on the City Council, had headed the Greater Philadelphia Chamber of Commerce, had been active in numerous civic activities, he had never put forth a clearly etched image of himself. He seemed aloof, but he really wasn't. He was intelligent, but not intellectual. He appeared gangly but was really quite an athlete. With no one else to turn to, Longstreth became the darling of the liberals. But he wasn't a liberal. He prided himself on his knowledge of city government, but his own track record on City Council was lackluster. (The only bill he introduced that got wide publicity was one to prohibit the sale of products made from the skin of American alligators. The Democratic Party majority on council laughed it into oblivion.) He considered himself a popular politician but he lost the 1955 election by 130,000 votes and was the party's second—perhaps third—choice to run against Rizzo. Arlen Specter, the popular district attorney, could have had the bid again for the asking. He wouldn't take it even when he was begged. Also, a number of knowledgeable Republicans thought handsome young Thomas Foglietta, a councilman from South Philadelphia, would be a better choice than Longstreth. But William A. Meehan, the GOP chairman, opted for the man known variously as "Daddy Longlegs," "Mr. Softee," and "Goofy."

To help clarify matters and to begin chipping away at Rizzo's granitelike image, Longstreth hired one of the most creative advertising men in town, thirty-two-year-old Elliot

Curson. Curson had helped elect Arlen Specter district attorney and Tom Gola city controller in 1969 with the effective campaign slogan: "They're Younger, They're Tougher, and Nobody Owns Them."

But Longstreth posed a different problem.

"What can I say about his argyle socks?" Curson asked. "These are the clothes he wears; this is the guy, what he has to offer. He's tougher? He's not the kind of tough that Frank Rizzo is. He's not a young man, he's a grandfather with four grandchildren."

There was, however, a ready-made issue—race. Curson thought he attacked it subtly with the slogan that finally emerged: "You Know He'll Do a Better Job."

"The slogan is based on the fact that surveys proved if it wasn't for the race problem, that some people are against the blacks, they would vote for Longstreth." Curson said.*

Two of the thirty-second, $1500-a-shot television ads Curson developed also hit directly at Rizzo's vulnerable points.

One showed Longstreth moving through a crowd, presumably at a Rizzo rally. "The Democratic machine knows if it runs on its record, they'll lose," he is shown saying. "They're trying to take your eye off the ball . . . by pulling you apart. But Philadelphia doesn't want a police state."

The other showed Longstreth standing in front of the Roundhouse, warning voters that the campaign was not to elect a police commissioner but a mayor, and that he was better qualified to hold the latter position.

Rizzo had his own ad man, another ex-*Bulletin* reporter. Ken Mugler, who, working closely with Gaudiosi, developed ads that reflected the low-key nature of the Rizzo campaign. The philosophy was to soft-sell Rizzo, to remind voters that here was a "proven product."

Mugler hired the deeply modulated voice of Carl Weber,

* *Philadelphia Daily News,* September 29, 1971.

an ex-television actor who had done the "voice over" for the Volkswagen and Zerox anti-freeze ads. Typical of the Rizzo ads was one showing him weaving through a friendly crowd, shaking hands. The "voice over" intones: "Frank Rizzo loves Philadelphia. This is his hometown. He knows its people and problems as no other person does. Now Rizzo wants to be your mayor...."

Despite the lengthy position papers that his staff issued on such subjects as housing, welfare, transportation, and city services, Rizzo, in his public appearances, stuck mainly to the issues he knew would elicit a favorable response from his followers.

CRIME: "When I speak out now I'm a Fascist, you know, and I'm going to head a police state. Let me tell you this, we'd better all wake up. We're going to have to soon." Rizzo said he wanted to hire 2000 more policemen, legalize all gambling and make winnings tax-free, throw out the "lenient judges" who turn "wild animals back on the street," and have judges elected every four years rather than appointed.

THE SCHOOL SYSTEM: "I give Mark Shedd [the school superintendent] about three seconds. He ought to start making some moving arrangements right now. I'm not an educator, but maybe we'd better go back to the old way—remember, you wrote As for a week, Bs for a week, Cs for a week."

TAXES: "There will be no tax increases while I'm mayor because I don't believe people in this city can afford to pay any more taxes. We're going to run this city just like a good housewife runs her home, you know, you do with what you have."

THACHER LONGSTRETH: "He's the polarizer. He has taken the low road, this fellow from Princeton. He makes the statement that I'm the polarizer. Yet he tells people in the black community that he's a 'white stick of dynamite with a black fuse.' I tell you, if I were black I'd be insulted. He calls me

Fatso, Bozo, names like that, you know. Well, he's taking the same polls I'm taking and he's starting to panic. That's why he's taking the low road. I'm getting a little disgusted with him. I think he needs help."

These themes, or variations upon them, struck a responsive chord among those who paid money to hear Rizzo turn them on. He never read from a prepared speech; he would step before the microphone at a fund-raiser and begin patching his speech together, a piece here, a piece there, and it would fuse. In addressing a group of businessmen, he would stress the need for lowering business taxes, pointing out that while Longstreth was president of the Greater Philadelphia Chamber of Commerce, "businesses were closing down and pulling out right and left. Where was Thacher?"

Somehow, he would usually get around to talking about Mark Shedd, the need for more police, and on and on, occasionally throwing in a comment about the editorial writers who continually criticized him, or the newsmen who gave him "fair treatment."

On at least one count, Rizzo was right. Longstreth did take the "low road." But it was a direction he took out of necessity. Rizzo's support was anchored deeply in the race issue, although Rizzo himself never approached the issue directly. He ran on his reputation as a cop, a hard-liner on law and order.

Meehan put it this way: "The issue in this campaign? Everybody's talking around it. Everybody's suggesting what it is. Well, I'm going to tell you what it is. It's black against white, that's what Mr. Rizzo is trying to make it. He doesn't have the intestinal fortitude or the guts to say it in so many words, but you know it and I know it. If he didn't have that issue, he couldn't get enough votes to keep him warm. You could put all his votes in a telephone booth."

Richardson Dilworth saw it like this: "The Democratic campaign slogan, 'Rizzo Means Business,' means that Rizzo will keep the blacks in their place."

Longstreth continually harped on another Rizzo slogan, "Firm but Fair."

"Yeah," he said. "Firm to the blacks, fair to the whites." If these commentaries were politically motivated, a similar statement by the Reverend Leon H. Sullivan, the founder of the Opportunities Industrialization Center and the only black man serving on the board of directors of the General Motors Corporation, was not. Rizzo could scoff at charges of racism from such black leaders as attorney Cecil Moore, or Hardy Williams, or black militant Muhammad Kenyatta. But the Reverend Sullivan was the most respected black man in the city and had generally steered clear of politics.

"Should Mr. Rizzo be elected mayor of Philadelphia, we will unquestionably have a divided city: a city divided racially, ethnically, and sectionally; and Mr. Rizzo could not possibly bring the city together," he said.

Thus Longstreth began attacking Rizzo overtly by saying that his image as a tough, honest cop was vastly inflated and that he did not deal effectively with organized crime; and he insinuated that Rizzo was conducting a racist campaign which fed upon bigotry and hatred.

To this he added carpings that Rizzo was a tool of the Democratic machine, a puppet whose strings were pulled by aging hacks at City Hall, most notably Mayor Tate. "A vote for Rizzo is a vote to continue the same tired old government we've had for the past ten years," he said time and again.

The effect of all this castigating rhetoric was difficult to measure, but Longstreth had undoubtedly come a long way since the campaign began back in the summer. He had entered the race as a hopeless underdog and, through hard work and much expensive advertising, had turned it into a reasonably close contest. He had also benefited from a long string of endorsements by national political leaders and a host of local politicians and civic leaders.

But the one thing he had not been able to do was lure the former cop out of his cocoon. He attacked Rizzo viciously, accusing him of racism, cowardice, and of fearing to be exposed as a know-nothing. Short of slapping a glove across Rizzo's face, he had done all a man could do to pick a fight. Rizzo, who privately seethed in outrage, kept his public cool.

"Thach thinks he's going to draw me down to his level, but he's wrong," Rizzo said. "I don't blow my cool that easily. I'm not going to help his campaign by appearing on the same stage with him."

About the closest the two men came to a showdown occurred during a baseball-hitting contest at Veterans Stadium, a widely publicized event that underscored the capricious, often absurd nature of the campaign. For days, both men boasted of their prowess at the plate. They even took time out from their busy campaign schedules to sneak in a little batting practice. Longstreth won it with a considerable blast to the outfield; Rizzo had to settle for a hard-hit grounder along the third-base line.

Finally, the Rizzo campaign architects, realizing that their candidate's refusal to debate the opposition was hurting rather than helping their efforts, consented to a debate. Or at least that's what it was termed. The format finally worked out by news anchormen from the city's three major television stations was so stifling as to thwart any attempt at a free-flowing verbal exchange between the candidates.

The rules called for each candidate to make a two-minute opening statement. One minute was allowed each man for rebuttal. This was followed by a question-and-answer session, in which the three anchormen asked the questions and the candidates were given one minute to answer and thirty seconds for rebuttal. The final twelve minutes of the hour-long "debate" were set aside to allow Rizzo and Longstreth to question each other. Answers and rebuttals were limited to one minute. Two volunteers from the League of Women Voters acted as timekeepers.

For Longstreth, it was the high point of the campaign. Coming as it did on October 14, just slightly more than two weeks before Election Day, this was a confrontation that he had to win decisively to maintain the momentum he had been gathering since September. Given his decided advantages in forensics, it would be damaging for him to pull away even or with only a slight edge.

"Everybody expects me to bowl him over," Longstreth said. "So even if Rizzo does just a reasonable job, it will be in his favor. He's very fast on his feet and very good with one-liners."

Inhibiting as it was, the format of the debate provided voters with their first genuine look at Rizzo the candidate. Up to this point, few outside the entrenched Rizzo wards who attended his fund-raising functions had even seen him, let alone heard him speak to the issues.

Thus the stone was at last rolled back, exposing the man for whom this rather incredible uncampaign had been waged. If at first he seemed a bit nervous, it wasn't long before he warmed to the task. Excerpts from the hour-long debate set forth Rizzo's positions on most of the problems facing the city, his personal philosophies, and his sashay manner of speaking.

QUESTION—Mr. Rizzo, why specifically do you want Dr. Mark Shedd to go?

RIZZO—Well, I have been in schools; I would say I've been to more schools than the superintendent of schools during my career as a police chief. And I have watched the system that produces illiterates, functional illiterates, kids that are juniors and seniors in high school that cannot read and write. I have watched the complete authority get taken away from teachers, from principals, a one-man operation. I have watched and I have observed Superintendent Shedd permit permissiveness. No authority to the teachers. In my opinion, he has made a shambles of this school system. It's nothing personal. But I have watched this decline and in my opinion the one man responsible for it is the superintendent of schools.

LONGSTRETH (*rebuttal*)—The absurdity of Mr. Rizzo's persecution of Dr. Shedd, blaming him for all the problems of society inherent in school situations in big cities today, can best be paralleled by saying that his only suggestion is to fire Shedd.

QUESTION—Mr. Rizzo, Senator Hugh Scott this week charged that your election would be nothing more than quote, "Tateism," with a new face. Richardson Dilworth also this week repeated the much-heard charge that you are Mayor Tate's hand-picked candidate. After that you were quoted as saying Mr. Tate would be no part of your administration, and he will have no influence on you. Does that mean that you have quietly broken ties with Mr. Tate?

RIZZO—Oh, no. I will always respect Mayor Tate because when I was police commissioner, he permitted no one to interfere with the police department and that included politicians. He did not interfere himself. But I will stand on my own two feet. Now, as far as Senator Scott and Mr. Dilworth are concerned, they have one vote in Philadelphia and that means that the people of this city will decide who the next mayor is going to be. And I have great confidence in the people, because I know that, the people of this city know that, know that Frank Rizzo was not bossed and Frank Rizzo ran a police department without political interference. And I'm going to tell you, that was the first time in my twenty-seven years that politicians did not interfere with the operation of the Philadelphia Police Department.

LONGSTRETH (*rebuttal*)—Well, Mr. Rizzo has called Mayor Tate repeatedly "the greatest mayor in Philadelphia history," which I think is a pretty effective indictment of his judgment.

QUESTION—Mr. Rizzo, despite your law-and-order stand, you have been accused of being rather lenient on certain segments of organized crime. How do you answer the innuendoes by your opponent that you have had secret meetings with one Mr. Angelo Bruno?

RIZZO—Well, this is so ridiculous. Secret meetings. The meetings that I had with Angelo Bruno. Well, when he was arrested and brought to Police Headquarters. And the secret meetings that my opponent referred to were at Police Headquarters. Mr. Bruno was arrested by my men while I was the police commissioner. And as a result of that raid—he was consorting with mobsters from other parts of this state—valuable records were seized and I personally delivered them to the district attorney of Philadelphia. And as a result of the seizure of them records, Mr. Angelo Bruno went before a grand jury and will be cited if he doesn't answer these questions. That was the arrest that broke the back of organized crime in this city.

QUESTION—Mr. Rizzo, since you say that you will bring all the people together, there have been some black organizations which have come out against you in this campaign. Just how would you prefer to go about bringing them as members of the society and in one community to solidify their thoughts?

RIZZO—Well, most certainly we're going to, you know, get to talk to various groups in this city. And the black community will be part of my administration, as will all the other ethnic groups. We're going to, this is, you know, a country that my own heritage would not permit anything different. I come from a background where, you know, things weren't always just right. But again, we will bring all the people together because I have this ability, I'm a leader, not a follower.

LONGSTRETH (rebuttal)—Well, talk is cheap, Commissioner. Why is it that you never, never, never, campaign in a black area? Why is it that you have no advertising in a black area? Why is it that you have none of the black leaders in this city who have come out to support you? Why is it that you don't even speak to the problems that concern the blacks and that relate to the blacks?

[Rather than follow this up, the questioner turned abruptly to the subject of finances and taxes—Author.]

QUESTION—Mr. Longstreth, how can you document your insinuation that Mr. Rizzo failed to act on alleged improprieties on a section of Locust Street [known as the "Strip" which had a number of bars employing B-girls and prostitutes]?

LONGSTRETH—Well, I think it's quite obvious when the State of Pennsylvania has to come in with a handful of state troopers in order to get those places padlocked, in order to get some action there, that the man who is responsible for the police department in Philadelphia hasn't been putting very much arm on them in order to close things up.

QUESTION—What proof do you have in this particular instance when he was police commissioner, not now?

LONGSTRETH—Well, I'm talking about what's been going on the last three or four years. The clubs on Locust Street have been operating in their present unholy way now for about as long as anyone can remember. It didn't seem to make very much difference whether he was police commissioner or not, they kept right on operating that way, and still have until the state troopers finally came in and closed them down.

RIZZO—First of all, to set the record straight, the state police did not come in and padlock them or close them down; all they did was serve legal papers. But my record as far as Locust Street is concerned—I made hundreds of raids, myself personally led the raids. Now, the Philadelphia Police Department is not the licensing agency of the liquor places on Locust Street. The state is the licensing agency. Now, the state has the responsibility to close them down. The Philadelphia police have done their job and done it well. And I'm very—I was thrilled when the state police came in and closed them down, or attemped to.

QUESTION—Mr. Rizzo, the Committee for Information on the Judicial Process said that city government officials have no control over judges and the committee has been alarmed by some of your statements. Among other things you proposed placing limits on the terms of Philadelphia judges. Since the mayor does not have such powers, what prompted you to make such statements?

RIZZO—Well, I have been, I was the first man who ever spoke out and was critical of judges and I'm still critical of 'em. I believe that the reason for our tremendous increase in crime can be placed at the feet of the judicial system. I'll tell you why—criminal repeaters that are arrested over and over again, eight, nine, ten, as high as thirty times. Now all that's required to limit the, you know a—tenure of ten years in office in my opinion is too long, they should, you know—all we need is two successive sessions of the legislature and then a referendum to the people to reduce the tenure in office from ten years to four years. So that they will have to campaign on a record. . . .

QUESTION—But doesn't this bring more politics into the whole judiciary process?

RIZZO—Oh, no. I think that if a man has to run for political office every four years and put his record on the line, it makes it a little different. And I'm sure the people are going to ask Mr. Judge, "What did you do as a judge? And let's see your record."

QUESTION—Mr. Rizzo, why were all the major scandals that took place during the Tate administration, while you were police chief, uncovered by the district attorney and the grand juries, and not by you?

RIZZO—Well, right off, there was never a better relationship in this history of this city between myself and Arlen Specter. You know there was a difference in politics there, but we worked very closely and I'm proud of that association. And many of the scandals that were uncovered, I worked on personally, with the district attorney's people. And I have provided Mr. Specter a total of almost sixty policemen who are now working in his office. And I was available to Mr. Specter and I supplied manpower. In fact, there's Philadelphia policemen right now working with Mr. Specter. And I'm urging the news media, I want this done, I would like them to interview Mr. Arlen Specter, and ask him some of the questions that have been asked to me tonight. And I will rise and fall on Mr. Specter's answers. I have that much confidence in Mr. Specter. And by the way, if Mr. Specter was the Republican opponent, I would not have run as a Democrat, I would have worked for Mr. Specter as a police commissioner.

LONGSTRETH—Commissioner, we've had a pretty good time here tonight, I think. We've had a chance to really get to the point of things, and I've enjoyed this because for the first time now I've had a chance to have a confrontation with you. And I think that we ought to do this again. And I want to ask you, will you join me in three in-depth television debates: on, one, how to pay for the kind of city we all want; two, how to give all our kids a good education; and, three, how to make our streets safe again? Come on, Commissioner, now, right now, give me an answer. Yes or no, it's an easy one.

Rizzo—Let me say this to you, Thacher. You know the reason that I will, I'll answer all the questions to the news media, or to the people of this city, but not with you. Because, I am going to tell you, you know, nobody knew who you were before this election. You're getting a lot of publicity tonight. You know if you had done your job as executive vice-president of the Chamber of Commerce, you would have had the thing that I have, recognition factor. Nobody knows who you are, Thacher.

It ended there. The long-awaited debate was over and Longstreth's worst fears had been confirmed. As Rizzo left the studios of WCAU-TV and walked across the parking lot to the sidewalk, a woman driver rolled down her window. He ran over to shake her hands and they exchanged a few words.

"Did ya hear?" Rizzo yelled to his aides who were dodging traffic on foot. "She said she's a Republican, but she heard the debate and she's going to vote for me. Did you hear that?"

Little of what was discussed in the debate was new. Rizzo, through press conferences, speeches, and position papers, had touched on most of the subjects at one time or another, as had Longstreth. But Rizzo had proved he could handle himself under verbal fire and he had dispelled the issue that he was afraid to meet face to face with his opponent. The one new point developed by Longstreth completely backfired on him. That was the issue of Arlen Specter. Specter, a Republican, was co-chairman for the Longstreth campaign and would later become President Richard M. Nixon's campaign chairman in Pennsylvania. But here was Rizzo the Democrat saying he would "rise or fall" on Specter's assessment of his record as a police commissioner.

The GOP leadership was already irked that Specter was not vigorously boosting Longstreth, as they thought he should. The next day they sat by in frustration as Specter emerged to say that he fully supported Longstreth's candidacy and would work to get him elected, but at the same time confirming Rizzo's statement that they had worked together closely over the years. It was an embarrassing and damaging development for Longstreth.

On the face of it, Longstreth's chances of becoming the first Republican to occupy the mayor's chair in twenty years looked good. The Democratic Party was hopelessly split. The liberal element, headed by Congressman William Green and David Cohen, had defected en masse to the Republican camp. Most of the city's influential black leaders had also denounced Rizzo. It was generally conceded that the majority of the 53,000 new voters between the ages of eighteen and twenty-one would vote for Longstreth. The area of the city that could swing the election either way—the northeast—was still considered Rizzo land, but Longstreth was thought to have made some inroads there. He had also picked up some unexpected, active support from Tom Foglietta, the popular Republican councilman from South Philadelphia. No one thought for a second that Longstreth could carry South Philadelphia. But if he could trim Rizzo's margin there and in the northeast, and if the black voters turned out heavily, and if it didn't rain, just maybe . . . maybe.

Rizzo was as confident the day before the polls opened as he had been back in February when he officially started collecting his pension from the city. He had the white middle-class vote all sewed up. He thought he would have a landslide in the northeast. Labor leaders throughout the city had flocked into his camp. And Mayor Tate had made sure that most of the city's employees, some 30,000 of them, would pull the Democratic levers. Two months before the election, the mayor's labor negotiator was sitting with the leaders of the American Federation of State, County, and Municipal

Employees, attempting to hammer out a contract that would hold wages down. The city was already faced with a staggering deficit, estimated at $60 million. A fat settlement to the union, whose members were already earning more than their counterparts in private industry, would further bankrupt the city. With fully a week left to negotiate, Tate suddenly propped his elbows on the bargaining table and gave the union every dime it was asking for.

Most importantly, Rizzo had the organization behind him, a brigade of political hacks, committeemen, ward leaders, and tomorrow's politicians hustling on the hustings and getting out the votes. They had organized 8000 block captains who would knock on doors on Election Day and escort people to the polls. The labor unions had provided 1800 volunteer workers and a convoy of 60 vehicles to get voters to the 1700 polling places. Some 60 telephone solicitors would be dialing their fingers raw from early morning until the polls closed at 8 p.m.

Longstreth finally brought his incredibly grueling campaign to a halt at the Bridge Street elevated terminal, last stop on the Frankford-Market line. He stood there as throngs of commuters headed homeward, reaching out to shake one last hand.

Rizzo wound it up where it had all begun, at a night rally in South Philadelphia, a half block from South Rosewood Street. About 5000 of his faithful *paesanos* packed the street and sidewalks as firecrackers exploded and the South Philadelphia Fife and Drum Corps tooted, fluted, and clanged. The candidate visited the house that his father had sold thirty-two years ago and told its present owner, Mrs. Emmy Gentile, "It hasn't changed much. You've kept it nicely."

Back outside he made one last speech.

"Just a victory is not sufficient," he told the wildly cheering throng. "I want a tremendous majority. I want a mandate.

I want to show that if you take the low road like my opponent, it does not pay politically. You get murdered. Some of his acts have been those of a desperate man."

It was off-season at the South Jersey shore. The sunbathers were back home braving the wet, cold winds of the city, and the old biplane no longer carried its political messages. Longstreth had a new banner now. He unfolded it in center city on election eve.

"Weather Report—Today, Rain and Rizzos. Tomorrow, Longstreth."

He was wrong. Election Day was cold and miserable and by mid-afternoon the rains came, falling in a torrent at dusk. By 9 p.m., the day and the power belonged to Francis Lazzaro Rizzo.

IX

Does Anybody Here Really Want This Job?

Candidate Frank Rizzo had just completed a modest lunch, consisting of a ham steak, vegetables, two rolls, and as many manhattans. He was obviously contented, not only with the meal, but with his campaign, and he pushed himself back from the table about a foot and reached for a cigarette.

"I'll tell you what I'd like you to do," he said. "The first day I take over as mayor I want you to stand in the courtyard of City Hall and look up at the windows. You'll see briefcases flying out, papers . . .

"We're going to clean out the bureaucrats," he added with a deep-throated chuckle. "No more three-hour lunch breaks. No more expense accounts. They're not gonna know what hit them."

F R A N K R I Z Z O took over City Hall in a swashbuckling, unorthodox manner that, while at times confusing, was delightfully pragmatic. This was by design to the extent that his major campaign promise had been not to raise existing taxes or impose any new ones. But it was also born of necessity because Philadelphia, like almost every other major city in the country, was flat broke. Why he had made such a promise in the first place was a source of consternation to many of his staff and closest followers. That he reiterated it time and again only reinforced what they had known all along: he is unpredictable.

So it should have come as no surprise that four months into his first year in office, he succeeded in pushing through City Council a new tax, a two-dollar head charge on all passengers arriving and departing Philadelphia International Airport. This was later amended to three dollars for departing passengers only.

Rizzo inherited from his predecessor, James Tate, an army of 30,000 city employees and several hundred top-ranking bureaucrats. Neither he nor his staff, with the execption of his finance director, Lennox L. Moak, knew much about the internal operations of city government or what, if anything, to do about the ineptitude, inactivity, and corruption that were part of the inheritance.

But they lunged forward at once in what seemed to be a tireless effort to shake the city out of its lethargy and in this they were partially successful. Rizzo's first major undertaking, one that he accepted reluctantly, was an attempt to salvage the floundering plans to stage an international exposition in Philadelphia in 1976 commemorating the nation's two-hundredth birthday.

He balked at the task because it smelled of death and he didn't want to be blamed for the fatality when rigor mortis was already setting in. But as chief executive he had little choice, and having once committed himself, he almost pulled it off.

For more than ten years, the city had toyed with the idea of hosting the bicentennial celebration. It was no coincidence that this span of time coincided with the tenure of James Tate. In the final analysis, Tate must shoulder much blame for the debacle, because by his bungling he allowed the committee that had been charged with overseeing this fete to wallow disgracefully in its own incompetence. Some $3 million was spent developing outrageous plans, and the only substantive result was a commitment from President Nixon that Philadelphia would, indeed, be the host city.

The main problem had been to find a suitable site on which to hold the international exposition. After long years of planning, the original Bicentennial Corporation came up with a pie-in-the-sky scheme calling for the expo to be held on a platform which would be built over the large complex of Penn-Central railroad lines at 30th and Market Streets. The estimated cost was a conservative $1 billion—about four times the absolute maximum the city could hope to obtain.

Understandably, the plan fell flat on its face no sooner than it was announced, and from that point on the bicentennial did a slow walk to the grave.

One of Rizzo's first moves was to reorganize the unwieldy, one-hundred-twenty-member committee and name a bicentennial site-selection committee. He also formed a new Bicentennial Corporation and between them, the two organizations began taking the first steps toward developing some realistic plans. But time and politics were not on Philadelphia's side. After picking three other sites, which eventually had to be abandoned because of local community resistance, the site-selection committee announced it had discovered the absolute, final resting place for the expo.

It was do or die in Eastwick, a swampy, foul-smelling tract of city-owned land in southwest Philadelphia, bordering International Airport. Eastwick served as a mosquito breeding ground and a cemetery for junked cars. Its unsightly appearance had always embarrassed the city fathers because it was the first parcel of city land a visitor or tourist using the airport would see.

Rizzo accepted the decision of the site-selection committee

and endorsed the final report of the Bicentennial Corporation —a detailed breakdown of transportation and other facilities that would have to be built and their costs. In all, the corporation projected the total cost of an international exposition in Eastwick at roughly $250 million. There remained but three steps to wrap it up. First, the plan would have to be approved by the American Revolution Bicentennial Committee, a panel appointed by the President to plan the nation's two-hundredth-birthday celebration. Then it would have to be approved by the Bureau of International Expositions in Paris. Finally, the President would have to give his stamp of approval and persuade Congress to appropriate the necessary funds.

Thus in April 1972, Philadelphia, after years of senseless procrastinating and bickering, finally came forth with what was, despite some inherent difficulties, a workable bicentennial plan. It would have taken a massive effort to pull it off, but it could have been done. That, at least was the opinion of Montreal officials who had put together a successful world's fair in 1967 in spite of similar obstacles.

Rizzo had done a creditable job in delaying the death of the expo. He had made the project a priority item in his first months of office and had devoted a great deal of his own time and that of his staff in putting it together. Of course, he had distributed some spoils along the way. For example, Al Gaudiosi, his campaign manager, had refused to move into the city from his suburban Lower Merion home; therefore, he was not permitted to work for the city. Rizzo solved the problem by appointing him public-relations director of the Bicentennial Corporation at $35,000 a year. City politics being what it is, the appointment was something less than extraordinary. Gaudiosi was eminently qualified for the position, anyway.

On the face of it, the city's chances looked fairly good. President Nixon only a few weeks before had reiterated to

Rizzo personally his position that Philadelphia was the bicentennial city. Demands by the Department of Commerce that the city come up with detailed plans for the expo had been met, and there was, if all went according to schedule, enough time to stage the whole affair by 1976. Suddenly, however, things began to sour.

The ARBC was scheduled to meet in May and make a final decision on the plans it would submit to Nixon. A few days later, the Bureau of International Expositions was to meet in Paris and vote on the site for an expo in 1976, presumably Philadelphia. The United States Embassy in Paris had confidently printed invitations to the foreign nations, requesting their participation. But several days before these crucial events took place, David J. Mahoney, the chairman of the ARBC, announced that the fate of the Philadelphia expo looked bleak because the cost (which he set at $1 billion) was too high. Mahoney said he favored not having a single focal point for the bicentennial, but allowing each state to hold a smaller celebration. His cost projections included the completion of a number of federal highway and transportation projects on which the bicentennial hinged, but which had been planned years before. They would be built with or without an exposition in Philadelphia.

Rizzo and some of his key planners rushed off to Washington to meet with Mahoney and John Ehrlichman, Nixon's urban-affairs adviser. Mahoney stuck to his guns and Ehrlichman said the President would abide by the ARBC's decision. The Philadelphia expo plan was dead even before the ARBC meeting for two obvious reasons and an unmentioned third.

It was during this period that the North Vietnamese launched their major offensive against the South; Nixon had reacted by stepping up the air war and throwing up a blockade of key North Vietnamese harbors. It would strain credibility to speak of celebrating American independence and international good will while at the same time taking measures against the North Vietnamese that could push the major powers to the brink of war.

Second, 1972 was an election year and Nixon's advisers felt there was political mileage in distributing federal bicentennial money into each each of the states rather than dropping the entire bundle into Philadelphia.

And finally, some federal and state officials were apprehensive about the ability of the city to provide adequate control over the large amounts of money that would be flowing through its business community.

These factors, combined with the fact that even $250 million might be hard to squeeze out of Congress during an election year, all contributed to the demise of the city's plans to hold an international exposition. What might have been a crowning achievement for Rizzo, an event that would have done much to revitalize and rehabilitate one of America's great cities, died a political death. Democrat Frank Rizzo, who had hailed Republican Richard Nixon as "one of our greatest Presidents," had failed at one of his first major undertakings. But he did not have to shoulder the blame, as he had originally feared, nor should he have had to. Besides, Philadelphians have come to expect these things.

Less than six months after taking office, Rizzo had come face to face with the harshest of all realities in managing a big city. Philadelphia was flat broke, if not bankrupt, and no amount of zealous leadership or stern austerity programs could alter the fact to any significant degree.

His first operating budget approved by City Council was set at $883 million; it included, despite prohibitions in the City Charter against deficit spending, projected revenues of only $772 million. The Philadelphia School District submitted to City Council a budget of $370 million; it carried a deficit of $60 million. Neither of these budgets included pay raises for employees, which were then being negotiated.

"I knew things were bad," Rizzo said at a news conference, "but I never realized they are as bad as they really are."

Rizzo took several steps toward solving the budget problem. He put a freeze on all city jobs, hoping through attrition to "trim away the fat." After six months of refilling only what he considered to be key positions, the payroll had been reduced by 265 people, which represented a saving to the city of approximately $250,000 a year—a relatively insignificant sum. Finance Director Moak checked his figures and concluded that further cutbacks would mean a reduction in basic services provided to the city's citizens. So much for that.

Then he began canceling contracts with consultants to the city, particularly lawyers. The first to go was the firm of Dilworth, Paxton, Kaliesh and Levy, which had been billing the city approximately $200,000 a year. This Dilworth, of course, was the very same Richardson Dilworth with whom Rizzo had been fighting for years, and Rizzo called a news conference to announce the action gleefully.

The contract, for an undetermined amount, was given to the firm of Blank, Rome, Klaus and Comisky, in which City Council President George X. Schwartz had been a partner until the preceding week.

"The switch speaks for itself," the mayor said.

Rizzo also pulled the rug from under David Berger, a Democratic attorney who had unsuccessfully opposed Arlen Specter in the 1970 election for district attorney.

Berger had earned about $180,000 in fees during a two-year period when he handled antitrust cases for the city. Rizzo gave this work to his city solicitor, Martin Weinberg, who set up a special city division to take care of it. This saved the city money because city lawyers work on a salary basis instead of on a percentage.

Berger had been Jim Tate's candidate, and it was Tate who had given him the lucrative contracts with the city. On one rather incredible contract, Berger stood to earn $2.49 million as his share of a $22-million antitrust suit against plumbing supply firms charged with price-fixing.

But these and other similar moves had little real impact on the budget deficit. Rizzo was counting on $60 million in federal revenue-sharing money, which, by summer, looked as if it might get through Congress. He had also requested an additional $165 million in direct aid from the state, which had no chance of being granted. Rural legislators in Pennsylvania are convinced that Philadelphia really isn't so bad off. At a State Senate Appropriations Committee hearing in Philadelphia, a Cumberland County senator asked Rizzo quite seriously, "You don't actually have many people earning less than $5,000 a year, do you Mayor Rizzo?"

The senator needed to look no further than out the window of the State Office Building at Broad and Spring Garden Streets in Philadelphia where the hearing was being held to see the faces of some of the nation's most poverty-stricken people.

Facing a poverty budget himself, Rizzo decided on a different tactic. Since the City Charter prohibited deficit spending, he set out to change the charter.

The City Charter was last revised in 1951 as an outgrowth of the reform movement spearheaded by Joseph Clark, then mayor, and Richardson Dilworth, his successor. Many of the revisions approved by the voters that year were aimed at strengthening the office of mayor and rooting out the corruption that had become institutionalized during more than half a century of continuous Republican control. While most civic leaders agreed that some changes were in order after twenty years, few were willing to go as far as Rizzo.

Even before he took office, Rizzo said he wanted the charter amended so that public officials could be elected for an indefinite number of terms. So, stymied by a lack of money, Rizzo and his staff began considering a number of proposals that would give him more power and more room to maneuver.

Rizzo wanted to do away with the provision of the charter calling for city contracts to be awarded on the basis of bids. This, he said, was needed so that only the best products could be purchased, not those merely meeting the uniform specifications that were sent out to various bidders.

Understandably, he came under heavy fire. Critics said it would open the door to corruption or, at the very least, leave it unlocked. Others, like Dilworth, said the mayor was attempting to build a dynasty.

Rizzo's reply to Dilworth: "Everything he has been with has gone down. Even the *Andrea Doria*." (Dilworth and his wife were aboard the vessel when it collided with another ship and sank in 1957.)

So heavy was the flak that Rizzo began retreating.

Initially, he had intended to place several members of his cabinet on the eleven-member Charter Revision Commission, which he was to appoint jointly with Council President Schwartz.

Then he decided to let Schwartz make all the appointments.

"I'm giving the ball to him," the mayor said. It was a dubious gesture since Schwartz was closely allied with Rizzo.

Finally, with newspaper editorials zinging him at every turn, Rizzo attempted to play down the importance of changing the charter.

"It's not all that earth shaking," he proclaimed. "There's no rush."

Rizzo doesn't seem to be happy unless he is "taking on" an adversary or engaging in a running feud with someone whom he considers to be his enemy. During his first months in office, he kept himself occupied in this department by swapping jabs—and occasionally roundhouse swings—with Governor Shapp and State Attorney General Creamer.

Shapp had alienated Rizzo during the mayoralty primary by endorsing Rizzo's chief opponent, Congressman William Green, Jr. During that same period, Creamer had walked into the fray by resurrecting police brutality charges against Rizzo that had been discarded seven years earlier. These antagonisms were heightened in November 1971, when the *Inquirer* began publishing a series of articles on alleged police corruption in Philadelphia.

With the exception of his wife and children, there is probably nothing dearer to the heart of Frank Rizzo than his beloved police department. His reaction to the *Inquirer* series, which raised more questions than it answered, and the subsequent move by Creamer to begin probing alleged corruption, was predictably angry.

The mayor vehemently denied there was "widespread and systematic" corruption throughout the 7500-man department. He charged the *Inquirer* with sloppy reporting and Creamer with "grandstanding" for the news media.

"J. Shane Creamer never successfully prosecuted anybody in his life," Rizzo charged at a news conference. "I invite you to look at his record. He couldn't carry Arlen Specter's fountain pen."

For his part, Specter had set up a special grand jury to investigate the alleged corruption and succeeded in bringing charges against twenty-five policemen. Then he moved against Greg Walter, an *Evening Bulletin* reporter, who had been investigating the matter with some assistance from Creamer's men. Specter had Walter arrested on wire-tapping charges.

Specifically, Specter charged Walter with taping his own telephone conversations with other parties without seeking their consent, a practice employed by the Philadelphia Police and Fire Departments. Indeed, Rizzo—denying he had even discussed the Walter case with Specter—said he would not instruct the police department to discontinue the wire-tapping.

According to Specter, Walter had been attempting to "set up" or bribe Philadelphia policemen, and there were many who accepted this explanation, including the mayor. But there were also those who thought that Rizzo and Specter had used the incident to embarrass Creamer, their old enemy, and ultimately Governor Shapp, as well as to discredit the investigative efforts of the *Inquirer*. Almost daily, Rizzo or Creamer or Specter would hold a news conference to lash out at one another. The performance resembled a circus side show more than a serious effort on the part of either side to deal with the problem.

The most apparent difference between the Rizzo and Tate administrations was one of style. A master of public relations, Rizzo brought with him to City Hall the open manner he had displayed at the Roundhouse.

Despite the fact that his relations with the news media at City Hall are considerably more strained than they were at the Police Administration Building, Rizzo remains a very accessible public official. He holds weekly news conferences, answers questions sent by readers in a weekly column in the *Inquirer*, and makes guest appearances on numerous television and radio shows.

Reporters have little trouble getting into the mayor's office. If not immediately available to answer a telephone call, he will return it as soon as possible. Under Tate, City Hall was a relatively quiet and peaceable place. Bureaucrats were inaccessible, either out to lunch, in conference, or absent. They reflected Tate's own personal manner, distrusting the press and shying away from reporters. Under Rizzo, City Hall is alive.

Rizzo himself usually works a ten- to eighteen-hour day, and he expects his staff and department heads to do the same. Executive lunch hours, the 12-to-3 p.m. confabs at downtown restaurants, are the rare exception. It is not unusual for Rizzo or the other top bureaucrats to eat lunch at their desks, and they have been able to transmit to the city at large the idea that City Hall is a place of intense activity.

For the first time since the Clark-Dilworth reform era, city government was generally thought of as being something more than a welfare agency for political hacks and bungling bureaucrats. Rizzo's common-sense approach to solving problems and his ability to relate to the man on the street on his own terms and in his own language gave him a credibility factor enjoyed by few politicians, least of all former Mayor Tate.

"I guess I'm best when I shoot from the hip," Rizzo confided during an interview. "They [his staff] keep telling me not to do it, but that's just me."

The net effect of Rizzo's presence in City Hall has been one of mood more than substance. There was a prevailing optimism, a feeling that the city was on the move. No one seemed quite sure of how fast it was moving or precisely where it was going, but that didn't seem to matter.

His administration had taken some positive steps at revitalizing a sagging economy. Harry Belinger, city representative and director of commerce, launched an ambitious program aimed at luring new business and industry into the city, no mean feat considering that Pennsylvania has an 11-per-cent corporate income tax, one of the nation's highest, and the city has a 3.5-per-cent wage tax, which frightens away high-salaried executives. The various department heads had attemped to get maximum efficiency from a large Civil Service corps that had traditionally been anything but hustling. And Lennox L. Moak, the finance director, had juggled every possible figure in an attempt to balance the budget.

"If we don't get the job done, it won't be from a lack of effort," Rizzo has said repeatedly.

During the campaign, Rizzo pledged to "bring the city together," meaning that he would ease racial tensions and attempt to better the lot of the city's more than 600,000 black citizens. His effect during his first six months was negligible. Despite his promise to appoint black cabinet members, the only blacks within the inner circle of his personal staff were three of his bodyguards, who were policemen. He did prove wrong, however, those who charged that he would bring down a reign of terror on the black community.

During the first few weeks in office, Rizzo made a determined effort at disarming the black teen-age gangs that had accounted for more than fifty deaths during the previous year. He called for a week-long moratorium on gang warfare and offered amnesty to any gang member turning in his firearms and weapons. The initial response was slow, but by the end of the seven-day period enough gang members had cooperated to prompt him to extend the amnesty period another week. The number of gang-related incidents and deaths dropped off sharply.

As spring gave way to summer in 1972, the euphoria that seemed to engulf Rizzo's administration during its first months of office disappeared. Despite the promises and the hard work his cabinet members had put in, Philadelphia still had critical problems which appear to defy solution. Some of the basic services such as trash and garbage collection had been improved to some extent, but there was no major expansion. The city still had an estimated 60,000 vacant housing units, high unemployment, a bankrupt school system, a deteriorated mass-transit system, inadequate health services, racial problems, and a rising crime rate. And Rizzo began to realize that his promise of no new taxes during his first four years would result in a cutback in services unless the federal and state governments pumped massive injections of money into the treasury.

Rizzo's own enthusiasm began to wane somewhat, not to the extent that it affected his work, but to the degree that he no longer attempted to couch the city's problems in bubbling rhetoric and meaningless platitudes. He had come to realize that his job was a near impossible one and that most of his work was conducted, by necessity, away from the public's eye. Rizzo seemed to thirst for the action of the streets, where decisions usually prompted results, as in police work.

During the campaign, Rizzo would respond to the question why he wanted to be mayor by saying, "Because I'm going to turn this city around," or, "I'm going to save this city." By the end of his first six months in office, he was considerably more restrained and decidedly more realistic.

"We do our best," he would say; or, "We're making a real effort."

Given the conditions under which he assumed running the nation's fourth largest city—the crushing financial burdens, the flight to the suburbs of the white middle class, the dwindling economic and tax base—Rizzo may be in over his head. The same could probably be said for any man. But for Frank Rizzo, a man whose ego and pride are overwhelming and easily bruised, the realization that he has "taken on" a foe more formidable than himself is becoming a painful experience.

Index

Opportunities Industrial Center, 180

Palumbo, Frank, 47, 156
Parrish, Ria, 113
People's Constitutional Convention, 85–86
Peruto, Charles, 144
Phelan, Frank ("Birdman"), 93–94
Philadelphia Bulletin, 156
Philadelphia Daily News: and Walter Annenberg, 126; and Tom Fox, 127; and mayoral campaign, 154–56, 164–66, and Rizzo's raids, 52, 59–60, 90; and "The Sounds of Philadelphia," 130; support of Rizzo's image, 119, 132
Philadelphians for Equal Justice, 88
Philadelphia Inquirer; and Walter Annenberg, 124–27; changes in ownership, 130–31; and Tom Fox, 129; and Hero Award, 58; and mayoral campaign, 143, 154, 156; and Rizzo, 57, 80, 108; 111*n.*, 120
Philadelphia Journalism Review, 123
Philadelphia Magazine, 44, 58, 72, 136
Powers, James, 75
Primary, Democratic mayoral, 140–68; and Rizzo, 140–68; and Tate, 148–49
Proscenium, The, 50

Quayle, Oliver, 16, 160–61

Rawls, William S., 87
Rizzo, Carmella (wife), 40, 111–12
Rizzo, Francis, Jr. (son), 111–112, 141
Rizzo, Frank: appearance of, 10, 30, 97–103, 112–13; early years of, 30–39, 44; and education problem, 15–16, 79–81, 106–107, 178, 182–83; as captain, 48–58; as deputy commissioner, 64, 67–8, 70, 74–77; as patrolman, 43–46; as Police Commissioner, 77–92, 104, as sergeant, 46–47; as mayor, 191–204; and mayoral campaign, 3–17, 11–12, 170–90; and popularity of, 7–8, 10, 16–17, 88, 102–104, 114–15, 127–28; and press, 44, 97–102, 116–39, 201
Rizzo, Joanna (daughter), 111
Rizzo, Joseph (brother), 7, 30, 37
Rizzo, Ralph (father): early years of, 24–26; death of, 40; influence on son, 29–30; 44, 46, 110; as policeman, 26, 28, 38
Rizzo, Teresa (née Erminio) (mother), 26–28, 39–40
Roberts, Samuel "Yellow," 35–36
Rosen, Harry "Nig," 35
Rosenberg, Samuel H., 45–47
Roundhouse, The, 74–78; 94–95; 122; 134; 141–42; 154
Rouse, Mary, 89

Savage, Philip, 87, 88, 89
Sayre, Nora, 123–24
Scanlon, Joseph, 147
Schoumacher, David, 108–109
Schwartz, George X., 197, 199
Schweiker, Richard S., 175–76
Scott, Hugh, 183
Selfridge, Robert, 97
Shapp, Milton J., 162–63
Shedd, Mark R., 79, 81, 106–107, 178, 182–83
Sloane, Judge Joseph, 84
Smith, C. Grove (Mrs.), 175
Smith, Elwood P., 90
Smith, Frank, 77, 146
SNCC, 76–77
Solomon, Morton, 97